EUROSOCIALISM
AND
AMERICA

EUROSOCIALISM AND AMERICA

Political Economy for the 1980s

Edited by
NANCY LIEBER

TEMPLE UNIVERSITY PRESS
PHILADELPHIA

Library of Congress Cataloging in Publication Data

Main entry under title:

Eurosocialism and America.

  Bibliography: p.
  Includes index.
  1. Socialism—Europe—Congresses. 2. Employees'
representation in management—Europe—Congresses.
3. Economic policy—Congresses. I. Lieber,
Nancy I.
HX238.5.E89   335'.0094   82-2014
ISBN 0-87722-273-8   AACR2

Temple University Press, Philadelphia 19122
© 1982 by Temple University. All rights reserved
Published 1982
Printed in the United States of America

Contents

Introduction

This volume grew out of the proceedings of a unique conference held in Washington D.C. in December 1980. The conference, entitled "Eurosocialism and America: An International Exchange," was sponsored by the Institute for Democratic Socialism and supported by a grant from the German Marshall Fund of the United States. Over 2,000 people attended the event, which was sold out in advance, and hundreds more were turned away at the door. Among the keynote speakers were past and future European heads of state and government—Willy Brandt, Olof Palme, Joop Den Uyl, François Mitterrand. Prominent American keynote speakers included Ron Dellums, Gloria Steinem, William Winpisinger, and Michael Harrington. In all, some fifty European socialist and labor leaders and experts came to participate in the conference as speakers, discussants and workshop leaders. Another dozen international guests (such as Guillermo Ungo from El Salvador, Felipe Gonzalez of Spain, and Bernt Carlsson of the Socialist International) came simply to show their solidarity.

Over two dozen American newspapers and journals covered this important conference (one notable, and unfortunately crucial, exception was the *New York Times*). European press coverage was more extensive and ran in over four dozen German, Swedish, French, Austrian, Swiss, Italian, British, Danish, and Dutch publications. Many of these articles noted that—on the eve of the Reagan administration—the conference constituted the largest socialist gathering in the United States since the 1930s.

Such publicity was welcome but secondary. The real purpose of this educational conference was to introduce the United States to the ideas and experiences of the social democratic, democratic socialist, and labor movements of Western Europe. To help accomplish this, a private meeting of experts preceded a larger, public conference. The former session was attended by some 100 policy makers and authorities from the American political, labor and academic worlds. The papers presented and the discussion that followed centered on three key issues of political economy in the 1980s: capital formation, industrial dislocation, and workers' participation. The larger public conference broadened the scope of the discussion and dealt with the political, social, and economic problems currently facing Western Europe and the United States.

Why was it felt that progressive Americans had something to learn from Western European socialists? Essentially, because of their past record. In the postwar period, Western European social democratic governments kept unemployment levels very low, distributed income more equitably, and saw their GNP per capita draw equal to, and (in the case of West Germany and Scandinavia) even surpass that of the United States. Contrary to prevailing American conventional wisdom and practice, these accomplishments did not stem from "trickle-down" economics, but from an expansion of government's role in economic and social matters. The Western European social democratic experience has proved that a higher standard of living can be achieved while providing extensive social services, stricter social regulation and control of business, and guarantees of workers' participation in management decisions.

Yet the Western European welfare states were not immune to the international economic crisis of the 1970s; in fact, they too are in difficulty. Like the United States, they are experiencing stagflation (high unemployment and high inflation), de-industrialization (a phasing out of basic industries), increased economic competition from the newly industrializing countries, and the high costs of energy dependence.

Because of these failings, Western European socialist and labor movements have been forced to reexamine the old social democratic verities and solutions. In many cases they have developed innovative programs to meet the challenges of the 1980s, programs which may have relevance to America's economic difficulties. The conference, then, presented the possibility of introducing "new" ideas into the American political debate—ideas that are commonplace (and often attract majority support) in Western Europe, but that are little known in the United States.

The book opens with an overview of Eurosocialism by Michael Harrington. Parts I, II, and III present the democratic socialist perspective on three key issues of political economy in the 1980s: capital formation, industrial dislocation, and workers' participation in management. They pose a common question. That is, are there alternatives to private, capitalist economic decision-making that are democratic, decentralized, and socially oriented? For example, can capital be raised and then invested to create jobs that are socially useful as well as profitable? Is there in fact a capital shortage (justifying business tax cuts and other incentives) or simply misallocation (capital used for speculative rather than job-creating purposes)? How can industrial and technological progress be channeled in a way that advances, rather than displaces, the lives and skills of workers? Who is to pay the social costs that result from private economic decisions regarding plant closings and the introduction of robot technology? How can workers achieve "full-time citizenship," which means control of their lives at work as well as during nonworking hours? If we are qualified to self-govern, in the political sense, why should we not be able to self-manage, in the economic sense?

The answers suggested in the following essays directly challenge the dominant economic powers in our societies. They call for greater competition in the financial sector through nationalized, trade-union, or cooperative banks and through the imaginative use of workers' accumulated funds (wage-earner investment funds in Europe, union pension funds in the United States). They entail democratically planned national or European-wide industrial policies, a new international economic order in which the multinationals are subject to greater public control, a larger role for the State and nationalized industry, especially in the advanced technological sectors, and much greater emphasis on a "social dialogue" between workers and managers. Finally, they call for working people to take part in making economic decisions, not only those concerning basic work conditions, but also those concerning the most complex questions of investment, relocation, personnel policies.

Because economic democracy directly assaults "traditional management prerogatives" (the rights of ownership and control), these and similar proposals have always been fiercely resisted by the conservative capitalist opposition. Of course, it could be argued that that same opposition fought *all* progressive reforms of the present system. Ironically, social democratic reforms have proved generally beneficial to the capitalists. In brief, it happened this way: the welfare state emerged at the public's demand—and at the public's expense—in order to make up for the "diswelfare society" created by private enterprise. Human service industries, often the least profitable of enterprises, were taken on by the State to fulfill social needs, and usually ran at a deficit. The more lucrative production of material goods remained the domain of "free enterprise." Since the public and private sectors for the most part did not compete, private interests found this coexistence tolerable. And so it has been argued that by "humanizing capitalism," social democracy simply forestalled the transition to a more radical democratic socialist society.

Many on the democratic left came to this conclusion by the 1970s. Coupled with the international economic recession, which created great difficulties for the functioning of the welfare state, this realization explains the democratic socialists' intention to move "beyond social democracy" and achieve a real democratization of the economic sphere. The essays in Parts I, II, and III offer analyses of economic democracy by nine experts from the trade union and socialist movements of Western Europe and the United States.

Part IV of the book moves from the presentation of specific economic proposals to a general definition of democratic socialism itself. Such a definition is necessary, particularly in the United States, because of continuing confusion over the term "socialist." From the time of the Soviet Revolution, countries ruled by Communist parties have persisted in calling themselves socialist. This misuse of the term has benefitted the Right by helping to discredit genuine socialism, which is inherently democratic. It was the perversion of the word by Marxist-Leninist regimes that forced socialists to adopt the redundant label of "democratic socialism." From its early roots in the nineteenth century to today, socialism means the extension of democracy—of the democratic process— to all phases of public existence.

Democracy, or majority rule, means the possibility of political equality through the guarantee of basic freedoms under the law. It means the possibility of greater social equality through an end to discrimination, the assurance of equal opportunity to all, and redistribution to a certain degree of wealth and income. It means the possibility of economic equality through the replacement of limited, private control of the workplace and the market with democratic and public participation in the economic decision-making process. Either socialism is democratic or it is not socialism.

In the concluding section of the book, four prominent leaders of the European socialist movement—François Mitterrand, Joop Den Uyl, Olof Palme, and Willy Brandt—elaborate on this definition of socialism as the achievement of political, social, and economic democracy.

Lastly, it is a pleasure to acknowledge support from the German Marshall Fund on the development of this book.

Nancy Lieber
Executive Director
Institute for Democratic Socialism

EUROSOCIALISM AND AMERICA

1

Eurosocialism

An Overview

MICHAEL HARRINGTON

Michael Harrington has been called America's foremost socialist. For three decades he has observed and actively participated in broad movements for social change—liberal, civil rights, labor, feminist, minority, and socialist. He has written twelve books and countless articles on the political, social, and economic problems of our times. Currently he is the national chair of the Democratic Socialist Organizing Committee and president of the Institute for Democratic Socialism.

In this chapter, Harrington provides an overview of the Eurosocialist movement in the postwar period. In the late 1940s, the socialists stressed nationalization and central planning. They began the construction of the welfare state. But the 1950s saw a resurgence of capitalist efficiency and growth. Socialization of consumption (through income redistribution) rather than socialization of production seemed the best socialist response. When it became apparent during the 1960s that inequalities persisted, a new challenge had arisen: integrating the "counter-cultural youth" of the new Left. The 1970s brought new problems—stagflation, world-wide recession—that demanded new answers. Harrington notes that the Eurosocialists succeeded in all these stages, to the extent that they constantly questioned their assumptions and choices. It is in this spirit that the authors of this volume present their analyses of political economy for the 1980s.

EUROSOCIALISM:
An Overview

Michael Harrington

There is a Eurosocialist movement, the most important mass movement of the Old World, one with great relevance to the last two decades of the twentieth century.

An impressive assertion—or is it merely a literary flourish without much substance? Certainly Eurocommunism has—or more precisely, had—a certain coherence as the expression of revisionist tendencies within a well-defined Communist movement, and it emerged within parties sharing a precise ideology. But the socialist and social democratic movements of the Continent (and the United Kingdom) are tremendously varied in their histories, their programs, and their cultural contexts. In origins they are northern and southern, atheist, Lutheran, Calvinist, Methodist, Marxist and anti-Marxist. Under such circumstances, can one even argue that a phenomenon called Eurosocialism transcends, or even unites, all of these differences?

As the chapters of this volume make clear, there is no such neat coherence; Eurosocialism is a complex and varied reality. But there is also a common European socialist experience and common kinds of responses to it. All of the socialist political parties are part of the advanced capitalist West; all seek to alter and in some cases transform that advanced capitalism; all began as parties of the working class and have become multi-class political centers of the broad democratic Left.

Indeed, I suspect that Eurocommunism will turn out to be a more evanescent development than Eurosocialism, and certainly less important. For a brief period it was possible to argue that the convergence of revisionist ideas in the Communist parties of Italy, France and Spain—and a number of similar trends in both European and non-European Communist parties—had created a new political force in the world. But the first articles and books were hardly published before the French communists, under the disastrous leadership of George Marchais, headed back into a neo-Stalinist ghetto, and Santiago Carrillo, the leader of the Spanish Eurocommunists, found himself challenged within his own party by an orthodox, Moscow-oriented faction. Unquestionably the Italian Communist party was, and is, one of the most significant and innovative institutions of the world Left, but that hardly adds up to a global trend.

Moreover, it is important to remember—much Marxist-Leninist rhetoric notwithstanding—that the Eurosocialists, with only one exception, are the party of the European working class. The Italian Communist party, of course, is that exception (the French communists were another, at least from 1946 to 1981, the year in which their vote fell to 1936 levels and their proletarian strongholds defected to the socialists led by François Mitterrand). If, as we will see in a moment, the socialists are not simply *the* party of *the* working class, they are more clearly the heirs of Karl Marx and the tradition he inspired than are the European communists. This is true even though there is not a single Eurosocialist party which is officially Marxist.

This movement of socialists and social democrats went through a series of significant (and to a certain degree common) experiences in the post-World War II period. Indeed, the reader will understand the various contributions to this book only if he or she perceives that they are self-criticisms, reflections upon a difficult past, as well as analyses and proposals for the future. The chapters are written by men and women who experienced the Cold War and then detente, who were first surprised by the vitality of capitalism and then shocked by its weakness. They are the European creators of the welfare state, from the 1880s (when growing socialist strength forced Bismarck to adopt a part of the socialist program) to the present. And as these papers make quite clear they are also struggling with the crisis of the postwar welfare state, a development which took place in the 1970s and coincided with, and was partly caused by, the crisis of stagflation in all Western economies.

It is therefore of some relevance in an America confronted by the same crisis of the welfare state and stagflationist economy to hear sophisticated discussions of possible solutions which are based on an experience in economic and social planning that is much richer than ours. In order to allow the reader to understand the context from which these ideas emerge, I will briefly outline the evolution of Eurosocialism since World War II. There have been four rather distinct periods in that political evolution:

- The immediate postwar years, from the Nazi defeat to the intensification of the Cold War, a time in which European capitalism was reeling from the material and political defeats of the Second World War and in which socialism seemed to be on the ascent;
- The period of capitalist-restabilization during the 1950s, the Cold War, the "affluent society" and the welfare state, a time of socialist revision and soul-searching;
- The 1960s and the generational struggle of the old and new Lefts as well as continuing socialist attempts to redefine basic ideas;
- The crisis of the welfare state as a result of stagflation in the 1970s and the need to respond, not to capitalist success as in the fifties, but to capitalist failure and contradiction.

In a sense, the Institute for Democratic Socialism (IDS) conference on Eurosocialism and America took place at the end of the fourth period and the beginning of the next, though where that beginning leads no one can yet say. There is in these chapters a willingness to re-think cherished and established ideas, a sense of radical challenge. None of the participants claims to possess "the" answer to the crisis; democratic socialists have known for some time that there is no simple solution (they learned through bitter experience). But there is a sense of new directions, of possibilities as well as dangers.

The prospects for European socialism also seemed extremely bright at the end of World War II. Julius Braunthal describes this moment in his history of the Socialist International:

> The World War had been preceded by an economic crisis which had condemned millions of people in the great industrial states of Europe and America to the unspeakable poverty of many years of unemployment. The parties of the bourgeoisie had been impotent in the face of this crisis. They had also declared ideological bankruptcy, surrendered the humanitarian ideals of liberalism and betrayed freedom and democracy when they felt that the capitalist order of private property was menaced by the workingclass. In Germany, Austria and Italy, the capitalists had made common cause with fascism; in Hungary, Poland, Roumania and the Baltic states they had created semi-fascist dictatorships. They were in the judgement of many guilty of the catastrophe of World War II. In France and England, the bourgeoisie had sought to purchase Hitler's goodwill by endless concessions and in France it eventually capitulated before, and collaborated with, Hitlerism. Was it conceivable that the broad mass of the people would ever again trust their fate to the parties of the bourgeoisie? Or wasn't it logical to expect that the historic hour had come for the parties of the workingclass, the hour of the socialist era in Europe?[1]

Moreover, it seemed possible that the split between the socialists and the communists, a conflict that had weakened the entire movement in the period *entre deux guerres*, might come to an end. When Stalin dissolved the Communist International in 1943, Harold Laski, a British Labour party activist and leader as well as a socialist theorist, said that the event was "one of the most hopeful developments since 1919" for uniting the workingclasses of Europe and Asia.[2] In 1945 these trends seemed to be at work when the British Labour party decisively defeated Winston Churchill shortly after victory in Europe, increasing its vote by an incredible ten per cent over 1935 and winning 393 seats in parliament.[3] And in October of 1945, the combined socialist and communist vote in France reached fifty percent, giving those two parties, both of which were then in government, 311 out of 586 seats in the Assemblée Nationale.

Ideologically, the Eurosocialists in this period were generally inclined toward the Left—if leftism is defined in terms of the standard, pre–World War II commitment to nationalization and central planning. In France, for instance, Guy Mollet led a majority within the Socialist party (SFIO) which rejected Leon Blum's calls for moderation and insisted upon the "condemnation of all attempts at revisionism, all forms of imperialist exploitation and attempts to mask that fundamental reality, the class struggle."[4] That stance became all the more ironic in the 1950s, when Mollet and the SFIO became the very model party of centrist coalition under the Fourth Republic. And in Sweden, there was a similar turn to the Left as the socialists called for a more active state role in the investment process and for the extension of welfare state measures begun during the Great Depression.[5]

Moreover, the Labour Party in the United Kingdom was actually redeeming every single pledge of its 1945 election manifesto. The Labour government created the national health system, nationalized a number of industries, and generally extended the welfare state "from womb to tomb." Thus it seemed, as Braunthal said, that the socialist era was at hand in Europe.

It was not. First, the Cold War emerged as the dominant fact of world politics; any thought of socialist-communist unification or cooperation was out of the question. The Italian socialists led by Pietro Nenni had concluded a unity-of-action pact with the communists in the resistance movement in 1944 and maintained that relationship in the elections of 1946 when the Italian Socialist Party (PSI) became the second party of the nation. But in 1947 the right-wing socialists, led by Giuseppe Saragat, broke with Nenni and formed their own Socialist Labor party. There was a similar split in the Italian trade union movement.[6]

So instead of a re-united working-class movement there was a resurgence of hostility between socialists and communists. At the same time, this first post-World War II period revealed less than overwhelming mass support for a truly radical transformation of capitalism. Surveys in Sweden showed that even supporters of the Social Democratic party were only lukewarm proponents of more socialization.[7] And Ralph Miliband, a Marxist critic of the official leadership of the British Labour party, notes that from the end of

World War I on "it is no doubt mistaken to suggest a picture of popular revolutionary fervour as the basis for electoral support of left-wing parties."[8]

Indeed, there was an irony in this situation: the very magnitude of the left-wing surges in Europe after World War II revealed a changing class structure. In the orthodox Marxist expectation, capitalism would polarize into a massive working class and a tiny bourgeoisie with little between the two (Marx, who clearly had this point of view in the Communist Manifesto, was one of the first theorists to realize it was wrong; his later revisions of it, however, were never well-known). Instead, twentieth century capitalism saw a proliferation of intermediate strata—the "new middle class" prior to World War I, for instance, and the "new class" after World War II. Although most Eurosocialists after World War II regarded themselves as representing the working class, their victories were in fact won because of multiclass support.

Moreover, experience began to show that nationalization, far from being an inherently socialist policy, could benefit capitalists more than workers. Marxist theorists had been aware of that possibility prior to World War I, particularly when they assessed Bismarck's "state socialism," but at that time it surprised no one that a Bismarckian nationalization would help the ruling class. Now socialist theorists perceived a more dangerous threat: nationalizations carried out by working-class parties in the name of socialism could aid the bourgeoisie much more than the proletariat. Unprofitable enterprises had been taken over by the government and their incompetent owners compensated. However, the new state corporations were often bureaucratic, run by the very same people who had managed them before, and operated on a capitalist calculus; even when the nationalized firms followed a "social" pricing policy, the largest users of their goods and services—almost always giant private corporations—benefited more than working-class consumers.[9]

Finally, the Marshall Plan had something to do with the problems the socialists encountered (even though many socialists supported the plan). The United States' commitment to the restoration of the European economies after the war was primarily motivated by anti-communism. As befits the only Western industrial society without a socialist mass movement, America carried out that task by restoring European capitalism. Thus a combination of Cold War factors, unforeseen social and economic developments and the resurgence of European capitalism frustrated the leftist hopes of the Eurosocialists in 1945. That laid the basis for the next period in the history of Eurosocialism: the time of reassessment and revision in the 1950s.

If the Eurosocialists of 1945 underestimated the resilience of capitalism, the Eurosocialists of 1950–60 overestimated the changes which had taken place in that system. This was a period of postwar boom, of a tremendous upsurge in world trade, particularly among the advanced economies. The Keynesian management of the mixed economy seemed to offer the prospect of permanent growth, and therefore a growing surplus which could be used to implement social programs without requiring any basic changes in the structure of ownership and investment. And so in different ways almost all the socialist and social democratic parties of Europe came to perceive socialism as the democratic political control and reform of a crisis-free Keynesian capitalism.

Since my account of the development will be critical in the main, I should preface it with an important qualification. Those who revised the Eurosocialist program in those years were absolutely right that the movement could no longer content itself with repeating the verities—the now discredited verities—of socialism during the 1930s and the immediate postwar years. The class character of capitalism had altered; so had its economic prospects. Therefore the "revisionists," even though they moved too far to the right, were carrying out a *radical* critique of outmoded doctrines, while many of those who defended the "Left" simply chanted venerable slogans over and over.

Let me take three cases in point from this period: the British, German and Swedish.

When Hugh Gaitskill became leader of the Labour Party in the fifties, he was committed to a modernization of party program and structure. The man who did more than anyone else to formulate Gaitskill's tactic was Anthony Crosland. His book, *The Future of Socialism*, was an intellectual and analytic manifesto for the Gaitskill wing of the party. It was also very much part of the broader socialist trend I have just described. Here one encounters new socialist attitudes toward private profit, nationalization and efficiency:

The statement that production for profit gives a bad distribution of resources (caviar for the rich before milk for the poor)
is only a shorthand. What is meant is that production is
undertaken for profit; that the distribution of purchasing
power determines what is profitable; and that if this is very
unequal, then the wants of the rich will be met before the
needs of the poor. But if purchasing power is distributed
more equally, it becomes more profitable to produce necessi-
ties, and less profitable to produce luxuries. . . . But to-day the
redistribution of incomes, and the rise in working-class purchasing power, have banished the worst effect of production
for profit by calling forth a quite different pattern of output.[10]

Therefore it is not necessary to socialize industry in order to get
socialist results; the redistribution of income will force the capitalist market economy to be responsible and decent.

This is a particularly important discovery, Crosland would
say, because "not many socialists" are unequivocally in favor of
taking over "the next five largest industries, and so on ad
infinitum."[11] The postwar experience, Crosland quite rightly
argued, had demonstrated that nationalization was a much more
complex policy than had been thought: "Some of the anticipated
advantages did not materialise; while certain unexpected disadvantages emerged."[12] Thus the issue of social ownership was no
longer a matter of socialist principle, but an empirical question to
be examined on a case-by-case basis within the framework of a
significantly changed capitalist economy.

Furthermore, one now understood that efficiency was extremely important because it was a precondition of economic
growth. Giving a high priority to growth, he argued, "is
not, as some socialists curiously suppose, to accept a Tory
philosophy. . . . A rapid rate of growth . . . at least for the next
decade, so far from being inconsistent with socialist ideals, is a
precondition of their attainment."[13]

There is considerable truth in every one of Crosland's points,
yet I think the basic approach is fundamentally flawed. To begin
with, Crosland, and many other analysts of the "affluent society"
in the fifties (but not, ironically, John Kenneth Galbraith, the man
who coined the phrase), radically overestimated the degree of

income redistribution which had taken place under the welfare state. This was documented in the United Kingdom during the 1970s by the Royal Commission on the Distribution of Income and Wealth.[14] Moreover, the persistence of inequality was not simply a consequence of socialist policy failure but rather an outcome dictated by the very structure of capitalism itself. There are different degrees of distributed wealth in different capitalist societies at different times—and there are also systemic limits, both economic and political, to these variations.

When the investment function is assigned either to wealthy individuals or, as is more and more the case in late capitalism, to retained profits, insurance companies and pension funds, those at the top must be treated better than those at the bottom or else they cannot carry out that investment function. A socialist (or liberal) government can reduce profits somewhat, but only if that does not set off a strike of capital. Moreover, that limit is not an objective economic fact. The Western bourgeoisie has been claiming for the past half century that socialists and liberals have made the system unworkable. In Crosland's Britain, for example, the Tories behave as if the Labour party had carried out a Red revolution when in fact it put through intelligent and moderate reforms. There are, then, structural limits inherent in capitalism to the redistribution of income and wealth.

But these facts (and my interpretations of them) were not as obvious in the fifties and early sixties as they are in the stagflationist eighties when there is a decline in real income in the United Kingdom, the United States, and some of the other affluent societies. Crosland, like so many of the Eurosocialists of that time, over-responded to the changes wrought in welfare capitalism during a period of sustained boom. He assumed that these conditions would last into the foreseeable future, but they were undone in the space of about a decade and a half.

The German Social Democratic party (SPD) made similar revisions at a special congress held at Bad Godesberg in November, 1959 (called the "Godesberg Program"). That section of the program discussing economic policy began on an almost utopian note: "The second industrial revolution is creating the preconditions for a general living standard much higher than ever before and for the elimination of the need and poverty which still

oppresses many men." To fulfill that promise, the program continued, the economy "must be adapted to changing structural
requirements through planning."[15]

But then came the new, Keynesian emphasis. The government, the program argued, inevitably influences the economy; it
is not a question of whether the state will intervene, but who leads
in the intervention. Within this context,

> free choice of consumption and the freedom to change one's
> place of work are decisive elements, and free competition and
> free entrepreneurial initiative are important elements, of a
> social democratic economic policy. . . . Totalitarian coercive
> planning destroys freedom. Therefore the SPD is in favor of
> the free market where ever there is actual competition.
> Where, on the contrary, the market comes under the
> domination of individuals or groups, many measures are
> necessary in order to maintain freedom in the economy.
> Competition to the degree that it is possible—planning to the
> degree that it is necessary.[16]

But this thesis assumes, as Crosland did, that it is possible to
have a dominantly private economy and a socialist government
co-existing over a long period of time without basic conflict. In
fact, as I have already suggested, socialist governments are subject to private veto power so long as basic investment decisions
remain in private hands. In making this basic criticism I am not
arguing that the perspective of the Godesberg Program was
tactically wrong in the Germany of the late fifties and early sixties.
At that point the socialists were striving against difficult odds to
become a majority party. Since society was hardly in a revolutionary mood, many of the accommodations urged in the Godesberg
document may well have been short- and medium-run necessi-
ties—but they were presented as basic principles.

Indeed, I think the SPD was quite right to abandon any
pretense of an official party "Weltanschauung." The ties with the
Marxist past had become quite tenuous and, in any case, there is
no evidence that people who share Marxist values and analytic
methods will necessarily arrive at common political conclusions.[17]
In any case, the communist pretense at reaching a "scientific" and
"Marxist" policy is an obvious fraud: Moscow decides on the line

and party ideologists supply the appropriate quotations. Breaking with that particular Weltanschauung was thus a solid and principled move.

At Bad Godesberg, Herbert Wehner, an SPD leader who had been a communist long before, described himself as one of the "burned ones"—former communists who through a false and misunderstood radicalism brought bloody tragedies upon their own heads. Wehner seconded Kurt Schumacher, the SPD's first post-World War II leader, observing that it is a matter of indifference whether one arrives at socialist conclusions by way of Marxist analysis or the Sermon on the Mount. The values, and the way in which they are reached, are of enormous consequence; but it is wrong for the party as such to adopt any exclusive philosophic doctrine.[18] Wehner's comments, and the SPD's adoption of that point of view, was not simply a matter of setting the record straight. It had important political implications.

The postwar class structure, as I have already noted, had significantly changed from that of the twenties and thirties, and was radically different from that of the capitalism during Marx's lifetime. If the transformations were not as radical as Crosland and many like-minded socialists thought, they were of great political significance. If the socialists were ever to become a political majority, they had to reach beyond the ranks of the classic blue-collar, industrial proletariat. "This program," Wehner said quite openly, "is not in a narrow sense a labor program (Arbeiterprogramm)." By that he meant that the party no longer spoke exclusively for the industrial working class, that it now proposed to lead all those people who work.[19]

There was another political dimension to these changes. In Germany, religion as well as class was a major factor in determining political preference. Catholics were much less likely to vote socialist than Protestants. The abandonment of a formal Weltanschauung opened up the possibility—which became a reality in the sixties and the seventies—of reaching out to Catholics. A similar process took place in France where a union federation which began as a confessional and Catholic movement became an important element in the socialist resurgence of the seventies and eighties. But even if one grants the wisdom of many of these changes in the German socialist program, it shared the same overoptimism about capitalism apparent in Crosland's writings.

Most Westerners, when they think about it at all, imagine the Swedish socialist movement to be genetically and culturally moderate, a movement which, in the grip of some mystic national spirit, inevitably opts for class collaboration and compromise. The reality, as John D. Stephens and Walter Korpi have documented, is quite different. The relative strength of antagonistic social classes is the factor that explains much of Swedish politics, not its mystic spirit. Thus the Swedish socialist rethinking of the 1950s was, in some measure, more complex than the British or German.

To be sure, the Swedish socialists reformulated their programs as the British and Germans did. "While basic criticisms of capitalism were retained," Walter Korpi writes of the new party statement of 1960, "the programme received a liberal flavour. Socialization of the means of production was treated more or less as an emergency measure to be applied in areas where private enterprise had proved itself unworkable."[20] When the party had turned away from the demands for socialization which had been made right after the war, it came up with an "active labor market" policy which seemed the very quintessence of Keynesian social democracy.

Both the Swedish socialists and the union favored a "solidaristic wage policy" which would limit differentials within the working class and give disproportionate increases to the least paid. In pursuing that goal there were no exceptions for marginal enterprises. If they could not pay their way, they were to be phased out, a tactic which recognized the necessity of Sweden being competitive in the world market. But there were alternatives. If an enterprise would invest in modernization, or even new areas of production, and thereby create new jobs, it would receive subsidies; if an enterprise went under, the workers in it were guaranteed retraining and, in effect, jobs at least as good as the ones they lost. Under such circumstances, the unions were able to accept a certain measure of wage restraint in return for job security.[21]

But if the Swedish socialists reformulated their program along the lines of those in Britain and Germany, and if their central policy was to promote capitalist efficiency and growth as a means of providing a basis for the socialization of consumption (but not of production), can it be argued that they are an exceptional case? It can, because they were also promoting a massive pension program in which a funded pension system under public (democratic) control became a major investor in the economy. That was bitterly resented by the bourgeois parties on the grounds, which were fairly accurate, that it represented "a 'secret socialization' plan."[22]

Interestingly enough, this move in an objectively radical direction was adopted for what would be called, in traditional (and often irrelevant) terms, "right-wing" reasons. The Swedish socialists wanted to appeal to the growing number of white-collar workers. They envisioned the pension proposal as a reform that would achieve the support of the white-collar workers along with the blue, and they turned out to be quite right. Ironically, the use of funded pensions to help determine investment in the economy not only created a blue-white collar coalition, it also moved the party and the society to the left. Rudolf Meidner, who was a participant in many of these events, describes the most recent, and even more radical, successor of this approach in his contribution to this volume.

So the fifties and early sixties were a period of Eurosocialist revision which was both timely and necessary. At the same time, however, socialist theorists mistakenly assumed that the capitalism driving the postwar boom had established a trend into the indefinite future. In many ways the sixties and early seventies were a continuation of that ideological development. They form a distinct period, however, because in these years Eurosocialism faced a new generational conflict.

At the congress of the Socialist International held in England in 1969—I report on it as a participant, having been the head of the American delegation—the problem of the new generation was a major topic for debate. The leaders of postwar Eurosocialism realized that they might suffer a significant defeat if they could not find some way to reach out to the cultural explosion brought about by the new youth movement. They had been forced to respond to the modified class structure of postwar capitalism; now they had to deal with its changed demography.

Throughout the Western world of the 1960s, and in Japan as well, there arose a new political as well as social counterculture. Most of its members were the children of semi-affluence, young people who had grown up under economic and social conditions which, if not as idyllic as some of the Eurosocialist revisions suggested, were light-years distant from the Great Depression. It was also a time of expanding higher education in an increasingly technological society. College youth had once been (in Europe much more than in the United States) the contented children of the bourgeoisie. But now many of the bourgeois young were becoming critical of capitalist society; in addition, lower-class parents were beginning to send their children to the university for the first time ever.

In West Germany these changes led to the "extra-parliamentary opposition," an anarchistic mass movement of the young. Eventually the more political wing of that movement entered the Young Socialists of the SPD (the "Jusos") and adopted a tactic of "the long march through the institutions." Their intent was to generate structural change from within the socialist movement rather than in opposition to it. In France the explosion of May, 1968 nearly toppled de Gaulle; in Italy, a variety of Maoists, anarchists and Left Marxists began to attack the Communist party as much too moderate; in Sweden there were similar Maoist attacks, this time directed against the socialists.

But perhaps the most fascinating development in this history took place in Holland. The Dutch Labor Party (PVA) had been a classic European Marxist organization prior to World War II (more accurately, the Social Democratic Labor party, which played a crucial role in establishing the PVA in 1946, fit into that category). But in the postwar era the PVA ceased to be a party committed to "opposition of principle," deleted most references to Marxism from its documents, and became a typical Eurosocialist party of that period, committed "to incremental reforms and improving the condition of the working class in the context of a mixed economy."[23]

In the sixties the New Left appeared in Holland, and like similar movements around the advanced world it was Marxist in its rhetoric but very concerned with concrete environmental and cultural issues. At the same time, Dutch Catholicism grew suddenly more ecumenical. Previous to this, like various Protestant groups elsewhere, Dutch Catholicism had played a confessional role in politics which had effectively kept the Catholic workers out of the socialist movement. Indeed, the Dutch Catholics were the theological vanguard of Catholic revisionism and renewal inaugurated by John XXIII and the Second Vatican Council.

The leadership of the Labor party was remarkably undoctrinaire in facing this youthful challenge. Rather than attacking, even excommunicating, the New Left, the older socialists reached out to it. Patterson and Thomas summarize the resulting change:

The PvdA of the 1950s and 1960s was concerned with promoting economic growth, the construction and elaboration of a welfare state and establishing greater public control in a mixed economy and the emphasis was on parliamentary and not participatory democracy. The PvdA of the 1970s is skeptical about economic growth, more concerned about the distribution of wealth, and anxious to guarantee material welfare but also to improve individual well-being and the quality of community life.[24]

It can also be argued that the French Socialist party (PS) of François Mitterrand—certainly the most dramatic and striking success of Eurosocialism in the recent past—also became the center of the youthful energies which had exploded in May, 1968. In France, however, that process is less obvious since it took place during the creation of a new political party. The PS descended, of course, from *la vieille maison*, the SFIO, but its refurbished identity stemmed from its ability to appeal to new strata: the young, the educated and, as in Holland, the Catholics. With some significant exceptions, then, Eurosocialism in the sixties and early seventies shifted culturally more than it did politically.

This is not to say that politics and economics were unimportant during this period. In 1966 the British Labour party under Harold Wilson actually won a larger percentage of the vote than in its 1945 triumph (47.9 percent as opposed to 47.8 percent), and even though its parliamentary delegation was smaller than under Attlee (363 seats as opposed to 393), it commanded an absolute majority in Commons. Wilson placed a considerable stress on automation (that "second industrial revolution" referred to in the Bad Godesberg Program), planning, and income and wealth redistribution. But not only did this thesis assume that capitalist growth could be continuous and crisis-free, it also argued that Britain could play an independent, socialist role in the world capitalist economy.

Thus Wilson faced a problem which confronts any democratically elected socialist government in a capitalist country: capital strike, and capital flight, and also the pressure of international capital, in this case from the International Monetary Fund. Most of the bright hopes of 1966 were sacrificed to an orthodox defense of the pound. Here again the socialists underestimated capitalist strength, particularly its power as an international system capable of disciplining elected governments by means of controlling credit.

Although the Wilson experience demonstrated some of the problems to come, the early seventies seemed to belatedly confirm 1945 hopes for a "socialist era." By mid-decade, Labour was back in power in London, the SPD ruled in Bonn, the Swedes had won two elections under Olof Palme, the Austrian socialists were approaching an absolute popular majority, Mario Soares became the prime minister of post-fascist Portugal, the Socialist party of France was on the way to overtaking the communists, the Spanish socialists were in the process of becoming the second party in a newly democratic Spain, and there were other successes in Scandinavia and Benelux (Belgium, the Netherlands, and Luxemburg). In 1976 Willy Brandt was elected president of the Socialist International, and that organization, little more than a letterhead for some years, began an ambitious and largely successful program of reaching out to the Third World.

There was, I think, an ironic reason for that period of socialist success: capitalist triumph. And the defeats of the second half of the seventies—the victory of militant conservatism in Britain, the end of more than four decades of socialist government in Sweden, the defeat of Mitterrand's Union de la Gauche in France, Soares' loss in Portugal, and so on—were a consequence of capitalist contradiction and crisis. Stagflation undermined the classic Keynesian prescriptions for counter-cyclical policy, making it impossible to fight inflation with unemployment, and vice versa. And that destroyed the basis of many of the Eurosocialist policies. The event was widely interpreted as a turn to the political right; in fact, it was a repudiation of all incumbents who had benefitted from the the relative boom of the sixties and early seventies.

The essays in this book belong to a time of transition. The defeats of the late seventies have been absorbed; the challenge of stagflation has been acknowledged; and there are signs of growing Eurosocialist strength in a number of countries. This volume, then, is a work of reflection and revision, marked by an openness that has not always prevailed in matters of socialist theory. Compared to the years between 1945 and 1980, the reader will find a much greater emphasis on decentralization and participation; an increased awareness that growth is a necessary, but by no means a sufficient condition for socialist advance; a sense of structural innovation (collective profit sharing and collective capital formation); a determination to reach out to the Third World; a new sensitivity to both religious and cultural issues.

Most Americans think they know what socialism is. In fact, they confuse it with Stalinism or 1930s social democracy. This volume will demonstrate that the Eurosocialist history I have just sketched has led to insights and proposals which are relevant to the stagflationist economies of both the Eurosocialist continent and an (as yet) anti-socialist America.

Notes

1. Julius Braunthal, *Geschichte der Internationale* (Hanover: Dietz Verlag, 1971), 3:20.
2. Braunthal, 3:19–20.
3. William E. Patterson and Alastair H. Thomas, eds., *Social Democratic Parties in Western Europe* (New York: St. Martins Press, 1977), p. 148; see also Braunthal, 3:53.
4. Patterson and Thomas, p. 26.
5. John D. Stephens, *The Transition from Capitalism to Socialism* (London: Macmillan, 1979), pp. 135ff; Walter Korpi, *The Working Class in Welfare Capitalism* (London: Routledge & Kegan Paul, 1978), p. 87.
6. Karl-Ludwig Gunsche and Klaus Lantermann, *Kleine Geschichte der Sozialistischen Internationalen* (Hamburg: Verlag Neue Geselleschaft, 1977), pp. 120ff.
7. Stephens, p. 138.
8. Ralph Miliband, *The State in Capitalist Society* (London: Nicolson & Weidenfield, 1969), p. 98.
9. Michael Harrington, *Socialism* (New York: Saturday Review Press, 1973), chs. 9 and 12.
10. Anthony Crosland, *The Future of Socialism* (London: Jonathon Cape, 1956), p. 92.
11. Ibid., p. 466.
12. Ibid.

13. Ibid., p. 378.
14. Great Britain, *Report of the Royal Commission on the Distribution of Income and Wealth*, 2 vols. (London: HMSO, 1975).
15. Social Democratic Party (SPD), *Protokol* (Bonn: SPD, n.d. [1959 or 1960]), p. 17.
16. Ibid., p. 18.
17. Michael Harrington, *Twilight of Capitalism* (New York: Simon & Schuster, 1976), app. C.
18. SPD, *Protokol*, pp. 98–99.
19. Ibid., p. 100.
20. Korpi, p. 89.
21. Stephens, p. 139; Korpi, pp. 88–89.
22. Stephens, p. 179.
23. Patterson and Thomas, p. 352.
24. Ibid., p. 360.

PART I

Capital Formation

2

A Swedish Union Proposal
for Collective Capital Sharing

RUDOLF MEIDNER

Rudolf Meidner is a pioneer in the field of collective capital sharing and democratic control of its allocation. As director of the research department of the Confederation of Swedish Trade Unions (LO), he authored the "Meidner Plan," a proposal for wage-earner investment funds. Currently he is a research associate at the Swedish Center for Working Life (Arbetslivscentrum) in Stockholm and at the Science Center (Wissenschaftszentrum) in West Berlin.

In his paper, Meidner presents his idea of wage-earner investment funds. In contrast to individual profit-sharing schemes (usually management-instigated in both the United States and Western Europe), Meidner's notion is one of collective capital sharing in order to increase the capital available to an enterprise as well as to grant workers greater influence over the use of that capital. Under his plan, actual ownership of an enterprise would be transferred slowly (over a generation) to the wage earners themselves. Meidner believes that the Western European socialist and labor movements, as they demand a more equal distribution of income, wealth, and power, will all move in this general direction.

A SWEDISH UNION PROPOSAL
FOR COLLECTIVE CAPITAL SHARING

Rudolf Meidner

The issue of employees' participation in the formation of capital has been discussed all over Western Europe for a long time, not as an academic exercise, but as a practical problem: namely, how to make capital formation compatible with the social goal of a more equal distribution of income and wealth?

Part of the difficulty stems from the postwar situation of Western Europe, a period of reconstruction and rebuilding of the national economies. A restrictive wage policy was an essential element of this process. At the same time, however, wealth and power became increasingly concentrated in the hands of those who owned the means of production. As the spirit of "national solidarity" faded away, various ways in which workers might participate in the accumulation of capital were discussed by unions and supported by other groups (liberals and churches, for example). Profit-sharing schemes were considered an appropriate method of equalizing the wealth structure.

Profit sharing is both liberal and paternalistic in its origins; company profit-sharing schemes have been used for a century by benevolent employers in Europe and on the American continent. But gradually the idea has changed its character: the current goal is less to increase the loyalty and thus the productivity of the employees than to enhance social justice and increase the influence of the workers.

We can best follow the course of the debate in West Germany, a country with an enormous postwar accumulation of capital and a strong labor movement which advocated a "responsible," i.e., restrictive, wage policy for many years. There was clearly a German economic miracle, but at the same time a very unequal distribution of wealth. The German trade unions, not by chance, were the first to ask for what they called social funds, financed by company profits and administered by the unions. In the beginning of the 1970s, the German Trade Union Confederation (DGB) congress adopted such a scheme and the German Social Democratic Party (SPD) followed shortly thereafter. For a number of reasons the German labor movement dropped the idea and concentrated its endeavours on co-determination of a more traditional character.

General de Gaulle, in the spirit of the paternalistic traditions of his conservative movement, introduced a compulsory profit-sharing system in France in 1967. This system assigned no real influence to the unions, however, but rather was an expression of de Gaulle's ideas of harmony in industrial relations.

Other countries in Western Europe have debated profit sharing. For ten years the labor movement in Denmark has discussed a proposal called "Economic Democracy," a wage-earner investment fund, financed by payroll taxes, with a twofold task: to increase the workers' local influence in the firms, and to contribute to capital formation. Unfortunately, the present political situation in Denmark bodes poorly for the prospects of this scheme. More surprisingly is the fact that the conservative-liberal coalition in the Netherlands has announced a bill proposing a scheme for compulsory "excess profit" sharing and the formation of a number of funds, run by boards on which the unions hold a majority. True, the scheme is a heritage of the former socialist government, but the fact that a nonsocialist government sticks to these ideas indicates strong support for some kind of collective profit sharing. Most recently the Commission of the European Communities has published a report which argues that employee participation in productive capital formation constitutes an efficient approach towards greater justice in the distribution of wealth.

Prior to 1975 Sweden stayed out of this debate. The nonsocialist parties had advocated the old form of profit sharing in single firms. The trade unions had rejected these schemes. They believed them to be inconsistent with the principles of a solidary wage policy, the objective of which is to equalize the wage structure using the nature of work, not profitability, as the criterion for wage-setting. Profit-sharing schemes would enable high-profit firms to pay higher profit shares to their employees, thereby destroying the wage structure.

It is surprising that Sweden has been such a late-comer in the Western European debate on workers' participation in capital formation, but there are some cogent reasons. First of all, the Swedish trade union movement is exceptionally strong. Its members felt no need to add a profit-sharing system to its traditional and very successful wage policy. Second, Sweden is an advanced welfare society with a sharply progressive tax system, a solidary wage policy and a state-run pensions scheme built on collective savings. For decades most Swedes felt strongly that they had made great progress toward economic equality and social justice. There was no reason, people argued, to fight for additional redistribution of wealth. Finally, when union claims for strengthening the workers' influence in firms became an issue in the mid-sixties, the debate resulted in intensive labor law reform: within a short period the labor government forced through bills on workers' representation in executive boards, on co-determination on all levels of the firms, on job security, and so forth. Co-ownership as an instrument for increased labor influence was hardly mentioned as a possibility.

When the issue of employee investment funds cropped up in the mid-seventies, public opinion was taken by surprise. But as always in historic developments, the reasons why things happen as they do become more apparent after the fact. Let me give a few explanations for the seemingly sudden change on the Swedish scene.

Unlike the pattern in other countries, the chief motivation for establishing some kind of collective employee funds stemmed from union policy as such. For decades the Swedish unions had strived for a "rational" or "fair" wage structure, and they applied the solidary wage policy as an instrument to achieve this goal. Despite many setbacks the gap between high- and low-paid workers had narrowed considerably by the 1960s. But wage solidarity for the well-paid means simply wage restraint, and wage restraint in highly profitable firms means that the owners catch what can be called "the firms' unused capacity to pay higher wages." The problem for the unions was how to redistribute these "excess profits" to the low-paid. For many years there was no answer, but the problem had to be solved, if the solidary wage policy was to retain the support of the well-paid groups. High wage drift in profitable firms and a number of wildcat strikes reflected the unions' dilemma. This potentially divisive problem was the decisive factor behind the LO proposal for wage-earner funds.

But there are additional reasons, some of them linked to changes in the economic and social conditions of Sweden. After many years of optimism and economic growth, people became more concerned about job security. Full employment was no longer self-evident. Weaker businesses (the "marginal groups") were being squeezed out of the labor market, with the result that unemployment replaced labor shortage as a major social problem. Moreover, segregated labor markets, a well-known phenomenon in the United States for many years, developed in a country earlier characterized by a high degree of homogeneity. At the same time research findings revealed a continuous concentration of wealth and power in private hands. The multinationals in particular—the majority of them Swedish—were perceived as a threat to national goals. All these phenomena resulted in stronger union claims for more democracy in economic life and humanization of work.

There was also a change in the union view on the role of ownership in democratizing the economy. Labor as such was still regarded as the main source of workers' influence, but (following the tradition of earlier Swedish socialists) co-ownership of production became accepted as a possible way to strengthen workers' influence in economic life.

We have to keep in mind all these changing conditions if we are to understand why the 1971 Swedish Trade Union Confederation (LO) appointed a working group to investigate whether and in what way the trade union movement should commit itself to collective capital formation, which gives the employees increased influence over the development of industry. The group had three specific tasks: first, to amend the wage policy of solidarity in order to eliminate the excess accumulation of wealth by owners of highly profitable firms; second, to counteract the on-going concentration of capital as part of the economic process in a highly industrialized society; and third, to reinforce wage earners' influence at the workplace through participation in ownership.

The group's report to the 1976 LO Congress should be seen as an attempt to initiate a debate, not as a series of final proposals. The report suggested, however, that 20 percent of annual pre-tax business profits should be transferred to a number of employee branch funds. These profits should be issued by the companies in the form of shares ("wage-earner shares"), not cash, and must remain in each company. This is the crucial point of the proposal; the authors of the report argued that the right to sell individual shares would soon result in a new concentration of capital that would undermine the whole system. The voting rights of the employee shares should be jointly exercised by locals and branch funds, and gradually the control of profitable companies would pass to the wage earners and their organizations. The authors believed that tying the growth of the funds to profits would counteract the further concentration of wealth and power without undermining the solidary wage policy. Also, the funds obviously would act to increase workers' influence in their firms.

The 1976 LO congress did not discuss the great number of technical details involved; instead it issued a statement in which it adopted a few principles:

1. The fund capital ought to accumulate out of company profits, the essence of the scheme being collective profit-sharing.
2. The benefits of the scheme should accrue to all employees, regardless whether their employers are contributing to the funds or not.
3. The capital of the funds may not be withdrawn from the contributing firms; consequently, no individual is entitled to receive any part of the fund capital.
4. There should be guarantees that the local members influence the administration of the fund capital. Centralization and bureaucracy should be avoided.

This statement was issued in June 1976. Three months later a general election took place in Sweden. For obvious reasons the labor movement was not prepared for a fight on this issue and was almost defenseless when the non-socialist parties made the issue of wage-earner funds—which they preferred to call "union funds"—a main issue in the election campaign. The socialists were defeated after more than forty years in government. Although a ruthless anti-nuclear campaign launched by the largest bourgeois party was the main reason for defeat, it was obvious that the public felt uncertain about the issue of wage-earner funds. And uncertainty among the electorate on important issues is without doubt a negative factor in politics. This fundamental truth was thoroughly exploited by the non-socialist parties; no one can blame them for that.

What has happened in this area since 1976? The story is somewhat confusing, although the position of the trade union movement remains clear: the statement of the 1976 congress is binding until the next congress (1981). The Social Democratic party, during its congress of September 1978, decided that wage-earner funds are necessary for four reasons: to complement the solidary wage policy; to counteract further concentration of wealth; to increase the influence of employees by co-ownership; and to increase total savings and capital formation. The first three reasons are identical to those adopted by the unions. The socialists added the fourth reason, which they consider necessary for restructuring Swedish industry, thereby enabling it to regain its competitiveness in international markets.

The decision of the congress was preceded by a joint LO-Social Democratic Party report which advocated a combination of employee investment funds financed by company profits and "development funds" financed by compulsory wage-earner savings. The congress adopted the four motives, but refused to endorse the report and all its technical details. Instead, the entire question was submitted to a royal commission which is expected to report back early in 1981. In other words, the Social Democratic party wants to postpone its final decision until the next congress in the fall of 1981.

Meanwhile, a recent event has offered an excellent illustration of labor's argument that decisions in large companies should not be made exclusively by private shareholders. The board of the Volvo company, the largest enterprise in Sweden with 65,000 employees, had planned to initiate industrial cooperation with Norway, with the governments of both Sweden and Norway involved and the Volvo unions supporting the plan. But a minority of shareholders refused to accept the plan and it had to be cancelled. That was a convincing demonstration of the power of the capital owners to make decisions, even when these decisions may have negative consequences for the economy, for employment and for the development of communities and regions. Thus the capitalists have furnished labor with a good argument for its proposal to establish collective wage-earner funds.

Sweden is in the middle of an intense and confusing debate, and it is hard to predict the outcome. Yet it seems likely that some kind of wage-earner funds will be realized in the 1980s, in all probability as the result of a typically Swedish compromise that includes elements of various schemes. There are good reasons for this expectation, not least of which is the mere fact that both the LO congress in 1976 and the Social Democratic Party congress in 1978 have formally decided that some kind of wage-earner funds should be introduced. The combined efforts of the unions and the party constitute a formidable force in Swedish society.

There are other reasons. The propensity to invest capital is low among Swedish owners, which jeopardizes both employment and economic growth. Wage earners are willing to contribute to capital formation, but only if they are able to influence the way in which these funds—their own money—will be used. Meanwhile, the process of concentration in the Swedish economy is accelerating. Through mergers, large companies, most of them multinationals, are becoming increasingly dominant, with the result that binding economic decisions are being made by even smaller groups of private capital owners. Wage-earner funds could act as a countervailing power while simultaneously strengthening the wage policy of solidarity. Certainly the Swedish labor reforms have so far given unions little real influence over the private sector. Disappointed by these experiences, the unions may turn more enthusiastically to co-ownership.

Politically controversial and technically incomplete as they are at present, employee investment funds may in the future be a cornerstone of the Swedish Model, a welfare society whose goals—hopefully matched by its achievements—are full employment, equality and wage-earner solidarity.

3

Capital Formation in the Third Sector

Cooperative and Trade Union Banks

NORBERT WIECZOREK

Norbert Wieczorek is a Social Democratic Party (SPD) member of the German Parliament. Prior to his election, he was vice-president of the international department of the Bank für Gemeinwirtschaft (Trade Union or Coop bank).

In this chapter, he looks at trade union and cooperative banks as alternatives to both privately owned and state-owned banks. He outlines the historic link of these institutions to the socialist and labor movements in Europe and discusses the benefits they were able to deliver to trade unionists and consumers. He assesses their role in the West German economy today, and concludes that while they possess more of a social conscience than other banks, their policies are limited by the surrounding competitive, capitalist environment.

CAPITAL FORMATION IN THE THIRD SECTOR:
Cooperative and Trade Union Banks

Norbert Wieczorek

Germany has considerable experience with businesses which are neither state-owned nor privately owned in the traditional capitalist sense. It is easiest to discuss them by considering the role of the trade union movement in this type of business. But let us first turn to two other areas which are also exceptions to the traditional capitalist firm. The first area includes those companies which are owned and administered by the workers. This is a very small group, originating from two main sources. In some companies the owner simply gave up his ownership to the workers; this happened, for example, with some small firms in the textile industry and, on an even smaller scale, in automobile sales. Other companies were unsuccessful under their original owners and were subsequently rescued by a kind of workers' cooperative. As a rule this was not a cooperative in the technical and legal sense, but was simply based on the cooperative idea. One of these, which received a great deal of publicity in Germany, was a small glass factory which came into existence with the help of the German trade union bank. However, all of these businesses are quite small and play no significant role in their respective industries.

In contrast, the second group, the large cooperative movement including farmers and small businessmen in German villages and towns, has a strong tradition. The first cooperatives were founded as early as the last century, and they represent an important factor in the German economy up to the present day. They more or less dominate agricultural trade; in 1979, for example, there were approximately 8,200 cooperatives in this sphere, with an annual turnover of 66.6 billion DM. They are the primary factor in all aspects of German agricultural trade and have a strong base in German farming. This is also true of wholesale purchasing cooperatives for small retailers as well as of retailing cooperatives run by small businessmen. In this area there exist some 888 cooperatives with a turnover of 61.5 billion DM. As a single group they are by far the largest distributors of consumer goods in Germany.

There are also cooperatives in banking. This group may be divided into two smaller groups, the Agricultural Cooperative bank and the Volksbanken, or "People's banks," which cater to the needs of the small businessman. They include approximately 5,200 banks with assets of 254.3 billion DM (1979), and are thus one of the largest banking groups in Germany; however, they are not as centralized as the large capitalist banks. Nevertheless, this large sector, which in itself is not typically capitalist in the classic sense, has taken on more and more characteristics of capitalism. One main reason for this is a strong tendency to centralize all of the smaller cooperatives, with the effect that, although the small businessman to a certain extent remains the owner—a member of the board of the small Volksbanken and so on—his power is being absorbed more and more by centralized cooperative bureaucracies. This means that central decision-making is gaining importance, particularly in retailing enterprises, in which shops belong to cooperatives; the official owner, who is responsible for running the shop, becomes more or less an employee of the central cooperative. So a kind of cooperative originally based on self-reliance has been transformed de facto into something which fits the conventional structure of German industry and trade based on monopoly and oligopoly.

The third sector involves enterprises owned by the trade union movement. Its roots also reach into the last century. One of the four main enterprises of this sector is the Bank für Gemeinwirtschaft (BfG), the newest of the four. It was not established until 1958; however, smaller workers' banks were founded in the

1920s and as early as the last century there were small savings banks for German workers. The other three include an insurance company founded in 1912, another cooperative movement, unlike the one I spoke of earlier, dating back to 1845, which is involved in both production and retailing of food and nonfood consumer products, and a large housing construction company which was also founded many years ago.

Let us consider the role of these groups in Germany. First, the cooperative movement: the Socialist party originally opposed it, regarding the movement as politically too accommodating. However, there was strong feeling in its favor in view of retailers' high prices and the level of workers' wages. These cooperatives were run on a local basis, and their main task was to provide for workers' everyday needs. This functioned well for a long time, and there was a firm tradition on the part of the working class to buy goods from the "Konsum," as it was called in those days. Because of structural changes in retailing, however, as well as the emergence of large companies in the 1950s and 1960s, it became impossible to maintain these enterprises as they were. They have now given way to a very centralized organization. Last year (1978) they had a turnover of 12.5 billion DM and employed a total of 55,000 people. They are now in a position to compete with the other centralized cooperatives mentioned earlier as well as with private enterprises, large chain stores, and department stores. This has led to the loss of grass-roots support by working-class families, since they are no longer directly involved in the cooperatives' management. They still have some say, but it is relatively insignificant.

Like all retailers, the cooperatives have other problems. For example, it is difficult for them to maintain competitive prices and stay in business in residential districts where enterprises dealing in consumer goods are scarce; there is only small demand for their products. One area in which they have benefited workers is wages; they are the only group which is almost completely unionized and which pays union scale; many German retail companies pay less than union-level wages. The cooperatives also give their employees special benefits and do a great deal for apprentices, unlike other retailers in Germany. However, these are the only main differences aside from the fact that, through their very existence, they exert competitive pressure on capitalist retailers.

Let us turn to the Volksfursorge, the second-largest insurance company in Germany (1979) with life insurance assets of 11.4 billion DM and 1.7 billion DM in assets in other kinds of insurance. Volksfursorge life insurance was founded prior to World War I because it was at that time impossible for workers to obtain life insurance at prices they could afford. Thus they decided to found their own insurance company, an endeavor which has been very successful although they also have some problems similar to those of the cooperative movement. The main problem is that they are subject to strict regulation by supervisory agencies; they are thus unable to be as competitive in price as they would like. A second problem is competition. Because of Germany's declining population there is, of course, a great deal of competition in the insurance business. In spite of this the company has been able to do a great deal for its customers. Particularly worth mentioning is the fact that it was among the first to grasp the financial consequences of the increase in average life expectancy; it was the first to change the statistical basis on which its life insurance rates were computed, thereby giving its customers the benefit of much lower premiums. Since most of those insured by the Volksfursorge are members of the working class, it has the highest number of policies in Germany. However, since the average amount of these policies is much lower than in other insurance companies, the cost factor is correspondingly higher, which makes competition more difficult. In terms of employment benefits and wages it is similar to the cooperative movement; it is the leader among the insurance companies.

Workers' banks in Germany originally served a very narrow group and were more or less restricted to a particular trade union. After the war, to some extent as a result of American influence, nation-wide banking was not permitted in Germany, a situation which lasted until 1957 when some regional banks were allowed to merge. The BfG, as mentioned earlier, was established by the trade unions at the end of 1958; at that time its assets were only 2 billion DM, but by the end of 1979 they amounted to approximately 54 billion DM. It now ranks among the ten major banks in Germany and holds fiftieth place on the world banking list. This growth resulted from two factors, neither of which is mergers, as is the case with other banks. BfG's success stems partly from internal growth. In addition, the bank's business policy was based on an idea rather unique among trade union banks. The idea was to establish a bank which would serve the public as a whole and not just one trade union. And in fact BfG business with trade unions and their companies, the large groups mentioned earlier, makes up less than 10 percent of the total; this means that 90 percent of its business is done with the general public. The theory was that a bank must be large to be viable. First, a bank must have access to money markets and capital markets, which is not possible if it is too small. Second, a bank must have a large organization in order to be able to provide specialized services, because banking is highly capital-intensive in today's world. These factors led to the bank's growth, which was financed mainly through the bank itself.

It is interesting to consider the two major consequences of this growth for the trade unions as owners of the bank. Most important, BfG has always been in a position to provide German trade unions with funds. This means that there have never been problems in carrying out a strike in Germany, although this is very expensive in view of high strike benefits. Of course the trade unions do not have all of their strike funds with the BfG, which would be foolhardy. They have funds in other banks as well, but nevertheless this is an important factor as far as power is concerned and creates a kind of balance in a capitalist environment.

The second important consequence of BfG's growth is that it enables the trade unions to receive information about developments in German industry. This information does not deal with specific companies; this would be impossible since no company would bank with the BfG if it were afraid that information about it would be passed on to the trade unions. But that is not the important point. What counts is that the unions receive an overall impression of the economy as a whole at board meetings and that they are informed about what is going on in different industries. They can then assess not only where they stand as unions, but what is going on in other sectors of the economy as well.

In addition, the BfG has traditionally been a leader in employer-employee relations. For example, the BfG's average wages are 10 percent higher than those of other banks. This is due to its wage structure; the wages of the lower-income employees are higher than those of comparable employees of other banks, while managing board members, for example, are paid much less than board members of other banks. Not only the wages themselves differ, then, but also the wage structure on which they are based. The situation is similar for employee holidays. Thirty days of paid holidays is becoming the rule in Germany's banking sector, as it has been for all BfG employees for four years. There are other examples of leadership as well, such as the breakthrough regarding the use of microprocessors and their impact on working conditions in the bank; negotiations on this matter paved the way for other banks.

Another area in which the BfG has made a contribution is in aid to businesses which are in difficulties. It has achieved considerable success simply by assessing the requirements of each situation and, if there is a chance to do so, investing money and saving the business in cooperation with its workers. It has also done some international work in this area, for example by helping workers' and savings banks in Central America.

So much for the benefits to trade unions. Let us examine the benefits to the consumer. In a very competitive environment it is not possible for these benefits to be too high, but BfG has nonetheless been successful in enabling workers to obtain loans. Even twenty years ago it was impossible for a blue-collar worker to get an installment loan. Now he can get one at a reasonable cost. Another benefit involves banking fees, which are very high in Germany. Of all the large national banks, BfG offers the lowest fees. There are other examples as well, but these few are sufficient to indicate that there are still ways of remaining competitive in the banking sector.

Let us now consider a common problem for trade union interests: because they exist in a capitalistic, competitive environment, their room for maneuver is limited. The accumulation of capital within companies can only come from those companies' profits; trade union money should normally not be channelled in that direction. Profit would be permissible as seed money, but not for such things as operating costs later on. This means that it is very difficult to make a profit and still remain competitive in a capitalist market. In addition, if a whole industry has to overcome structural problems such as those experienced by cooperative retailing enterprises, it is a very costly matter to set things right again, which has a negative effect on trade unions in general. As long as some areas continue to be profitable, that profit can be transferred from one to another, but this would not be possible if all areas are affected by a stagnating or even declining economy.

Another major problem is that, because of the trade union background of these businesses, the ordinary worker is sometimes frustrated because he thinks his claims are not being given adequate consideration. He expects special benefits which these businesses cannot give him, or at best only to a limited extent. He is not directly involved in running things, because out of managerial necessity he is represented by the trade union hierarchy in the decision-making process of the companies, but he derives no satisfaction from that.

There is little grass-roots support to speak of; there is some, but less than one would expect. This is a problem for which there is, as yet, no clear solution. One way to nurture support is by paying visits to trade union meetings to explain problems to the members, but when difficulties arise it is all too easy for communication to be cut off. It is often difficult to obtain the support of the ordinary worker. However, a solution must be found if the challenges of the future are to be mastered. It is clear that enterprises in the areas of banking, insurance, and also construction and housing, have played a useful and constructive role for many people whose well-being we in the trade union movement have particularly at heart.

4

Toward Democratic Control of Capital Formation in the United States

The Role for Pension Funds

CAROL O'CLEIREACAIN

Carol O'Cleireacain is chief economist in the Department of Research and Negotiations for District Council 37, American Federation of State, County, and Municipal Employees (AFSCME), AFL-CIO, New York City.

In her paper she reminds us that union pension funds are one of the most significant sources of capital formation in the United States. They constitute, in fact, the largest single institutional shareholder in the country. Yet while unions technically own vast amounts of capital, they do little if anything to exercise their ownership rights—that is, to determine where these funds are invested. Since unions do not send representatives to sit on boards of trustees, professional investment managers handle these portfolios as they would any other—profits come first, social consequences last. O'Cleireacain concludes that pension funds, if and when they are consciously and politically controlled by the unions, represent an enormous reserve of capital and power for the progressive movement in America.

TOWARD DEMOCRATIC CONTROL OF CAPITAL FORMATION IN THE UNITED STATES: The Role for Pension Funds

Carol O'Cleireacain

Democratizing the control of capital in the United States involves making more democratic both the use of existing capital stock and the process of capital creation. For some people, of course, economic democracy in the United State is an academic exercise. For others, it is fundamental to the goal of trade-unionism. To others still, it is so frightening that legislation has thrust successive obstacles in its path. But there is no doubt that American capital markets today offer the *potential* for workers' control of their assets.

There are three main fronts on which to exert more control on capital: control of physical capital, control of finance capital, and control of the process through which the creation of new capital takes place. The first will be addressed by the chapters on dislocation and worker participation. This paper concentrates on the last two.

American workers already own, but do not control, a significant amount of capital: namely, their pension funds. There are two main reasons to focus on pension funds when looking for a mechanism to achieve democratic control of capital formation in the United States. First, pension funds play a central role in the financing and structuring of contemporary American capitalism.

They provide the bulk of equity and bond purchases. In the 1970s corporate pension funds alone bought more than half of all new equity issues. In a typical year pension funds provide about three-quarters of net corporate bond purchases. In 1977, for example, more than 50 percent of the $35 billion of net corporate bond purchases were bought by insurance companies, largely on behalf of pension funds; 15 percent were purchased by corporate pension funds, and 12 percent by state and local government employees' pension funds. In short, the data indicate that employee pension funds dominate the financial institutions and that financial institutions dominate the capital formation process.

Second, pension funds provide a unique opportunity for worker access to where investment decisions are made—the corporate boardroom. Labor could exercise control over those decisions commensurate with its degree of ownership of capital; workers' financial power could counter corporate financial power. There is a lot of worker financial power to wield: pension funds are the largest institutional shareholder, holding approximately 25 percent of the market value of the New York and American Stock Exchanges. This led Peter Drucker to comment that "if 'socialism' is defined as 'ownership of the means of production by the workers' . . . then the U.S. is the first truly 'socialist' country."[1] But, if we observe how pension funds actually operate in capital markets, it becomes apparent that "socialism" is not exactly what we have.

The Role of Pension Funds in the Financing of Capital Formation

Savings are turned into investment via a series of highly structured and specialized markets that are dominated by large institutions. As we all know, saving is both voluntary and forced. Of voluntary household savings, somewhere between one-fifth and one-quarter (about 22 percent) goes into insurance and pension fund plans. This becomes part of the pool of savings available to the large financial institutions who generally use it to purchase equities in or make loans to (buy bonds of) the largest 500 corporations. Of the remaining voluntary household savings, almost 40 percent goes into accounts at commercial and savings banks, where it largely finances housing, small businesses and durable consumer purchases; the remaining 25 percent goes into the direct purchase of corporate equity, although very little of this represents newly issued stock.

The main form of forced saving in the United States is pension fund contributions made by employers as a commitment to retirement income for workers:

> Part of the money not paid in contributions would accrue to the employees in the form of higher wages. Part . . . would be spent on current consumption. . . . In sum, (if there were no . . . pension system) consumption would be increased over current levels, while savings and investment would be decreased."[2]

These forced savings (or deferred wages) come under the management of large institutions—insurance companies, bank trust departments, or the corporate employers' own investment department—which funnel them into the traditional forms of "blue chip" investment.

Businesses save out of profits. They distribute some as dividends, but retain the rest. Historically, the corporate sector has financed the bulk of its investment from these retained earnings. Increasingly, however, retained earnings have decreased in importance as a source of corporate financing, being replaced by external forms of financing: equity; debt (bonds and bank loans); and state subsidies, such as tax concessions, loan guarantees, state development bonds, etc. Of this external financing, corporate debt is the single most important: of total capital expenditures by the non-financial corporate sector in 1979, just over 50 percent was raised in the credit market (given monetary policy, it was probably raised quite short-term).[3]

As recent work indicates, the credit market is not homogeneous, but rather a series of markets which match up the sources and uses of funds depending on region, liquidity and risk preference.[4] Large multinational corporations tend to go to national, even international markets for either equity or debt issues. Their issues tend to be large enough to defray the costs of underwriting and meeting the necessary public regulations. The high fixed costs of public market financing exclude smaller firms who rely on private placements and bank loans. The bond and equity markets are dominated by the institutions, the largest of which are pension funds and the insurance companies that represent pension funds. In the 1970s, corporate pension funds alone bought more than half of all new equity issues. Of the $34.9 billion of net corporate bond purchases in 1977, insurance companies bought $18.3 billion—virtually all through private placements; corporate pension funds $5.3 billion; and state and local pension funds $4.1 billion. Thus the pension funds dominate the publicly issued debt market, and the insurance companies, on behalf of pension funds, dominate the private placement market. The institutions are calling the shots to large and small firms alike.

These data indicate that pension funds are major participants in corporate financing. As such they are key in a system which in this century has increasingly seen the displacement of entrepreneurs by professional managers.[5] This formal separation of ownership and control of corporations (which Berle and Means noted as early as 1932) has become more pronounced:

> While stock ownership may have become . . . more widely distributed, *thanks to the dramatic growth of institutional investment, control of stock remained centralized* [my emphasis]. . . . As a result, the formal control of corporate stock was not substantially different in the 1970's from what it was during the previous century. Rather than being concentrated in the hands of those who owned their own corporations, it was now almost equally concentrated in the hands of those who administered stock portfolios.[6]

Even though the proportion of pension fund assets held as corporate stock has been declining since its peak of 65 percent in 1973, non-insured private pension funds continue to be the country's largest institutional stockholder, generally estimated to own 25 percent of the market value of the New York and American exchanges.

There is no public equity financing in the United States. Unlike Europe, the United States has neither government-owned enterprises nor tripartite investment advisory boards (such as Britain's National Economic Development Office). The AFL-CIO proposal for a tripartite "reindustrialization" investment board, financed by pension fund capital with a federally guaranteed rate of return, appears to be as far as American labor is willing to go at the moment along European lines. The emphasis on pension assets is typically American; so is the avoidance of any mention of a public equity component or who controls the investment decision-making.

To back up their proposal, the AFL-CIO documented the size and scope of pension funds. As Figure 4-1 indicates, assets now total $625–650 billion; although spread among some 500,000 plans, these assets are quite concentrated. For example, more than a third of all the joint-trusteed funds' assets are held by the ten largest funds (ranked by assets), and the top twenty-five corporations hold nearly a quarter of the total employer-trusteed funds. This is for a pension system which currently covers about 60 percent of all employed workers (55.5 million people), only 40 percent of whom are in the private sector.

All private sector pension plans—currently worth about $380 billion—are trusteed and subject to ERISA (Employee Retirement Investment Security Act) regulations. Under the Taft-Hartley amendments to the National Labor Relations Act (NLRA), the employer establishes the fund. The workers must demand and win participation in administration; if they do, it is jointly-administered. (Unions cannot be sole administrators of non-contributory plans.) However, at present only about $100 billion of these assets are jointly trusteed. Many unions have yet to win joint representation on pension fund boards. Of those who have, in both public and private sectors, few have exercised power (and then very rarely) over specific investment decisions. Few as yet have demanded the right to vote their corporate shares. In these series of abdications of economic power, American labor has in effect turned away, consciously or unconsciously, from exercising some influence over the major levers of capital formation in the United States: the sharing out of profits; the generation of new ownership; the creation of new debt; the size and location of new investment; and, ultimately, the management of the existing capital stock. Clearly, the minor involvement in these pension funds demonstrates the low priority unions have assigned to the control of capital. To some extent it also reflects the emphasis on current rather than future gains through collective bargaining.

Public sector pension plans—currently worth about $250 billion—operate under a variety of rules and regulations. The

FIGURE 4-1
PENSION FUND SIZE AND SCOPE

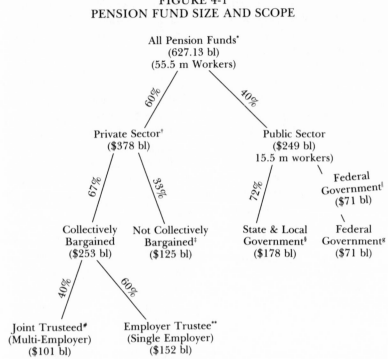

*   Dollar estimates, 1980. Employment estimates, 1978.
†   All of these are trusteed and covered by ERISA. 1970 BLS estimates are that
         79% are non-contributory for workers.
‡   Most of these are turned over to banks and insurance companies to manage,
         or the benefits are contracted to an insurance company directly. Large ones
         are likely to be managed "in house" by the corporate asset management
         department.
§   Virtually all defined benefit plans, subject to state legislation. They are *usually*
         joint contribution, with some worker representation on the controlling
         boards.
‖   Assets can only be invested in federal government securities.
Largely defined contribution plans, generally in the building and needle
         trades.
**   Largely defined benefit plans, bargained by industrial unions, such as the
         UAW, Steelworkers, CWA. (ERISA provides that even if unions do not
         negotiate joint trusteeships, they are entitled to disclosure of portfolio in-
         formation.)

Source: Jocelyn Gutchess, update of Ruttenberg et al., *AFL-CIO Pension Fund
Investment Study*, August 20, 1980.

assets of the Federal government pension system (about $71 billion) can be held only in the form of federal government securities (or cash). Most state and local government plans, although covered by IRS rules for tax-exempt status, are also trusteed under state laws, with standards and restrictions on trustee behavior varying from state to state.[7] Usually, employees have some representation on these trustee boards, but joint control is not guaranteed.

What is the present ability of workers to gain control over these assets? Of the total $627 billion worth of assets, about 35–40 percent ($220–$250 billion) are currently accessible.[8] In addition, there is almost $152 billion worth of collectively-bargained single-employer funds in either the private sector or the remaining state and local funds which currently have no employee trustees. Therefore approximately 70 percent of pension fund assets lie within present bargaining or legislative reach of workers.

To grasp their effect on investment, consider the annual flows of these funds. Pension funds are growing at an annual rate of about 11 percent. If approximately one-quarter of pension fund assets turn over annually, then new money (the 11 percent growth is about $60 billion) plus turnover ($140 billion) would finance about half of $400 billion gross private investment in the United States.

Ownership, Administration and Investment of Pension Funds

Who owns pension funds? There is legal agreement that pension funds represent workers' deferred wages, but their ownership is more complex than that of voluntary savings.[9] The assets of pension funds are held in trust and managed on behalf of the beneficiaries. Under fixed contribution plans, an individual worker can determine his/her share of the assets. Under fixed benefit plans an individual worker's claim on the fund is determined by his/her accumulated pension rights. The size of that claim depends on the benefit rules of the system and the job-rights of each particular worker. Many systems have such complex vesting, turnover, seniority and pay-related rules that determination of an individual worker's pension claim is extremely difficult. Although vesting and transferring among pension plans is easier than it once was, pension assets cannot be inherited and are highly illiquid.

Although individual ownership of assets held in trust at any specific time may be impossible to apportion, collective ownership rights are clear. A pension fund represents the deferred wages of all the workers who have ever been covered by the employer's pension scheme. There is only one mechanism through which those workers are able to voice their collective ownership responsibilities: through their representatives on the board of trustees. For collectively bargained plans, that representation comes from the union. In the public sector employee representatives are usually appointed to the board (from unions where there is collective bargaining). It is difficult to imagine workers in the non–unionized private sector winning representation on pension fund boards of trustees before unionization.

Trustees, who are legally responsible for pension funds, have two general functions: administration and investment. Both offer vehicles by which labor trustees can gain greater control over workers' assets, and can do so within strict fiduciary guidelines on administration and investment decisions.

Let us first consider administration. An important part of pension fund administration is the determination of the appropriate level of funding. For fixed-benefit plans, the sound actuarial level of employer contributions will depend on assumptions regarding future wage increases, death and disability rates, employee turnover, the rate of inflation, and the rate of return on the fund's portfolio. Variations in these assumptions yield a wide range of contributions. Since the employer contributions come out of current earnings, the contributions partly determine how much income will be left to distribute as profits, as wage and other benefit increases, or for use in corporate investment. The assumptions behind the funding decision, then, are complex. Labor is continually torn between the adequate funding of pensions and maximizing current wage and benefit increases.

As a matter of fact, considerable underfunding of corporate pension plans is common. It sometimes happens because newly negotiated increases in benefits are treated as unfunded liabilities, but it can also be the result of choosing assumptions which minimize, as much as allowable under law, current contributions. Through underfunding, the corporation manages to get the workers to incur the *risk* of not receiving a pension, since the corporation is making inadequate provision to meet its future liabilities.[10] Unfortunately, workers tend to overlook two important leverage points when such underfunding occurs: first, the ability to force the corporation to allocate profits to the pension fund; second the ability of workers to use those assets to exercise control over investment and capital allocation decisions. Joint trusteeship is a necessary but not sufficient condition for controlling both.

Theoretically, trustees control investment decisions. Current practice is that trustees set broad investment guidelines (portfolio mix) but leave day-to-day management of the funds to banks, insurance companies or their own corporate asset management departments. Such practice successfully separates ownership and economic control. The large financial institutions—banks and insurance companies—monopolize the control of pension fund investing. A recent study by the Industrial Union Department of the AFL-CIO (IUD) indicates that at least one of the top four pension fund managers—Morgan Guaranty, Bankers Trust, Equitable Life and Prudential—was used by 50 percent of the plans surveyed. That study even found several companies for whom Morgan served as a pension fund manager, principal creditor *and* stockholder as well as having interlocks with the board. The potential for abuse and conflicts of interest was well documented in the Twentieth Century Fund's study. Even under ERISA, it remains very difficult to prevent banks and insurance companies from "churning" accounts, giving differential treatment to clients, and dumping private placements of securities into pension accounts.

How well have workers' interests and financial assets been protected by those with the control over decision-making? Not well. In the 1970s, the average return on pension funds was 4.3 percent annually.[11] This was significantly below the rate of inflation. Compared to the 5.9 percent annual return for the stock market as a whole (using Standard and Poor's index), this difference meant a loss of about $1,000 per covered worker.[12] Measuring the return over other time periods yields results equally dismal, as Rifkin and Barber demonstrated. From 1967 to 1976 the market (Standard and Poor's index) grew 6.6 percent annually, while pension fund assets controlled by banks increased 4.4

percent and those controlled by insurance companies went up 4 percent. From 1962 to 1975, interestingly, 87 percent of all money managers performed below Standard and Poor's index. It is true, of course, that pension fund portfolios contain more than stocks. Bond portfolios have their own yardstick of performance. However, Standard and Poor's index is being used here as a benchmark of the average return on easily accessible and fairly liquid investments. Presumably, one advantage which large financial institutions could be expected to offer pension funds is their considerable wisdom on and experience of the capital markets. Yet they have failed miserably. To this writer's knowledge, unfortunately, these poor performances have never been seen as violations of "fiduciary responsibility."

Fiduciary standards affecting investment and capital decisions have been laid down by ERISA. Trustees ". . . must discharge their duties solely in the interest of the participants and beneficiaries and,

1. for the exclusive purpose of providing benefits and defraying reasonable administrative expense;
2. with the care, skill, prudence, and diligence under the circumstances then prevailing that a prudent man acting in a like capacity and familiar with such matters would use in the conduct of an enterprise of like character and with like aims [the prudent man rule];
3. by diversifying plan investments so as to minimize risk of large losses, unless under the circumstances it is clearly prudent not to do so.[13]

These rules have come to be interpreted by the layman as constraints on how pension funds may be invested. The "sole benefit" rule was meant to eliminate the possibility of self-dealing by trustees. Litigation on this issue has held the rule to mean that "in the consideration of the non-economic elements of a pension investment, economic self-interest may not play a role—it does not establish that other non-economic considerations may be ignored."[14] In a later case, when New York City chose to use its employee pension funds to prevent the city's default and bankruptcy—clearly a case with the potential of pitting current workers against retirees—the court ruled the judgment to be prudent.[15] The court's ruling has been interpreted to mean that such non-traditional types of investment are permissable so long as due deliberation and the considerations have been taken.

The "prudent man" rule (more appropriately termed the "prudent expert" rule) is often mistakenly interpreted as mandating minimum risk and maximum return. If it were to mean that, it would directly contradict the "diversification" rule. The purpose of diversification is to allow the spreading of risk across a portfolio. Modern portfolio theory indicates that the risk attached to any individual security can be divided into two parts: one which is correlated with the movements in the market; the other which is random. The random risk can be virtually eliminated through diversification of a large portfolio, leaving only the market-related risk. The Labor Department's administration of ERISA recognizes this (even if many pension fund managers do not), by leaving prudence specifically unrelated to risk and by allowing for judging individual investments within the context of the entire portfolio:

> generally, the relative riskiness of specific investment . . . does not render such investment . . . either *per se* prudent or *per se* imprudent, and, (2) the prudence of an investment decision should not be judged without regard to the role that the proposed investment . . . plays within the overall plan portfolio. Thus, although securities issued by a small or new company may be a riskier investment than securities issued by a 'blue chip' company, the investment in the former company may be entirely proper under the Act's 'prudence' rule.[16]

Investment decisions are made with regard to the entire portfolio. The only two relevant characteristics in making the choice are first, an investment's expected rate of return and, second, some measure of the risk of realizing that return. The risk is measured by the variance of the expected rate of return, that is, the probability of the expected rate of return actually being achieved. Portfolio managers recognize that a trade-off exists between the expected rate of return and risk. A simple example: the desired return to be gained by investing can be generated three different ways. One way combines some probability of success and some rate of return. The same return may be generated by a higher probability of success and a lower expected rate of return. It may also be generated by a lower rate of success and a higher rate of return. Portfolio diversification sees a role for all three combinations, diversifying both risk and rate of return. *Trustees often consider only the first two combinations, refusing to recognize that high risk investments have a role in a balanced portfolio. So long as they can demonstrate the potential for a high rate of return should they succeed, a plan for worker ownership of a failing company, such as that proposed for Youngstown Sheet and Tube, cannot be considered as violating fiduciary prudence.* A relatively painless way for pension funds to engage in such high risk ventures would be to create a special pool, made of small contributions of individual pension funds, specifically for high risk investing. With such a pool there could be some diversification of risk; at the same time, no individual worker or single fund would have so much at stake.

It is reasonable to expect that forays into social investing would initially involve projects which offer no additional risk or sacrifice of return. These are simply the easy ones. There is nothing prohibiting the investment of pension fund assets in "non-traditional" types of ventures, so long as decisions are made carefully and according to established procedures. Unions have begun to recognize this; the UAW has moved step by step into a program of "social investing" at Chrysler, including divestiture, housing and geographic targeting. The contruction unions have for some time used the AFL-CIO "J for Job Program" to target investment in the unionized construction sector. Various public sector unions have been active in supporting geographical targeting in the investment of public employee pension funds. Finally, then, there is recognition of the possibilities that differ from the "blue chip" securities on which advisors have concentrated and which have yielded such disappointed returns. Traditional investment management has persisted undoubtedly because it is easiest in terms of information and handling the secondary market. It serves the interest of the financial intermediaries; it is how things have always been done; and it has not been opposed.

Not only have the financial institutions failed to deliver a reasonable rate of return on pension fund assets (thereby generating unfunded liabilities and lower than necessary employee compensation), they have been allowed to act as if they themselves owned whole sectors of American industry. For example, the "power to vote stock in 122 of the largest corporations . . .

represent[ing] 41% of total market value . . . is concentrated in 21 institutional investors."[17]

Although financial institutions are not terribly open about their attitudes and procedures in exercising the voting rights which accompany corporate shares, they appear to adhere to the so-called "Wall Street Rule." Under this rule, the institutional investor does not take an active role in pressing for change in the corporations; rather it passes the proxies to management. If it feels it cannot give such a vote of confidence to management, it sells its shares. To quote Harold E. Bigler, Chairman of Connecticut General Life Insurance Company's investment advisory subsidiary, which oversees the $14.5 billion of assets ($2 billion in equities) of the eighth largest life insurance company:

> The master trust agreements for 7 of our 8 Investment Advisory Accounts make no mention of proxy voting; therefore the trustees have the right to vote the proxies unless they chose to pass that right on to us. The trustees of 5 of these accounts have . . . passed them on to us. Two . . . clients do not . . . break down . . . holdings. . . . Therefore we do not vote proxies for those accounts. In the 8th instance the client specifically states that . . . [we] vote proxies. This client also requests that we inform him, on a timely basis, whenever we vote against management.[18]

This is not to say that the large institutional investors have no control over the corporate sector. Rather, they choose to exercise this control through creditor relationships and placement of sympathetic persons on the board of directors instead of using stock proxies.

By abdicating their stock ownership rights, pension fund trustees have chosen not to exercise control over deciding who sits on the board of directors. All key capital formation decisions flow from the boards; they determine the rate of profit retention, the rate of borrowing, the rate of share issuance, the location of plants, and the rate of net investment. The implications of these decisions on traditional labor-management relations are well recognized by American labor; and labor has not wanted to bring those issues to the boardroom. But, what has generally gone unrecognized is the rightful place in the boardroom which comes to workers from their ownership of corporate shares (and more indirectly from their role as corporate creditors through the bond market).

What about conflict of interest of labor representatives on boards of directors? Legally the board serves in a trustee relationship with the shareholders (owners). Any member of the Board, then, is bound to represent the shareholders' interest. But how broadly or narrowly defined is that interest? It is certainly broad enough to encompass the points of view which span the cross-section of shareholders, among whom are workers whose group interest or collective involvement with ownership is the determining feature of the holding of corporate shares.

The Social Democratic Use of Pension Funds

Several European countries have gained greater democratic control over capital formation in a manner similar to that recommended here: by using their pension fund investment and stock ownership rights. The approaches of Denmark and Sweden are worth examining briefly. The trade union movement in both countries clearly recognized the role of pension funds in the capital market[19] and made a conscious effort to use workers' assets to pursue at least several important goals: they wanted to promote economic growth that encouraged exports, and they wanted to move beyond co-determination to co-ownership.

In 1977 Danish unions agreed in a compromise round of bargaining to the formation of a Special Fund which would receive foregone cost-of-living increases. It is governed by a twenty-one person board made up of fifteen wage earners and six government appointees. The board's ability to invest funds is constrained by the following guidelines: a maximum of 20 percent of the assets may be in equities, so long as the fund does not own more than 20 percent of any one company; the remaining assets must be in bonds, loans to municipalities or cooperatives, and housing. These investment rules are less strict than those governing Danish pension funds.

In addition, the Danish health workers' pension funds (PKA) received new "social" investment guidelines in January 1980. These aim at increasing the share of equities in the portfolio to the full 15 percent allowed by law, and focusing that ownership in such ways as to generate unionized jobs in Denmark, preferably with export-oriented growth firms in which co-influence with the company is possible.

In 1973 Sweden established a Fourth Fund. Like the Danish Special Fund, it is not a pension fund which must make annual payments to workers. Until the change in government, its resources came annually from the three main Swedish pension plans (usually 1 percent of their contributions). It is strictly an investment fund, operating only in the equity market. It is governed by an eleven member board which draws five of its members from the unions, two from private employers, two from municipalities, and two from the government. Governed by rules which mandate a sound return, no investment in banks or insurance companies, a maximum of 10 percent ownership in any one company and, initially, restriction to new issues, the fund has grown to 2½ percent of the Swedish capital market. It holds stock in a quarter of the 140 companies listed on the Swedish exchange, is the largest shareholder in three companies and the second largest in twelve. As such it has moved to elect its candidates to fourteen boards of directors. Interestingly, its candidates are, generally, national figures sympathetic to workers' interests; they are never Fourth Fund directors.

The Danish and Swedish approaches must be placed in the political and social context of the basic European model of social democracy. Both countries enjoy a high degree of trade-union authority—Sweden's labor force is 90 percent organized; Denmark's 80 percent—and the trade unions are highly centralized, with national rather than local bargaining. There are national wage, price and income agreements among labor, employers, and the government in welfare states which actively redistribute income—from property owners to wage earners, from higher wage earners to lower earners, and from all workers to the retired and the young. Labor representatives sit on boards of directors (co-determination), and both countries have a labor party, that is, a formal political arm for the trade unions. Finally, the state takes an active economic role in the allocation of capital through regional and industrial policy.

How Do We Begin to Move in Their Direction?

The United States has a very different set of institutions. First, its federal structure has resulted in corporation laws, labor relations, taxation, subsidies, and interest rates that vary widely from state to state. This has encouraged businesses to migrate in the past. Second, the American labor movement is not in a position of strength. It lacks an effective centralized structure; its proportion of the American labor force is low by developed countries' standards, and declining; it is not actively expanding its base; and it has difficulty delivering the votes of its members. Third, there is no political party which backs the democratic control of capital. The absence of a labor or social democratic party means that strategies which require government policy must continually be based on negotiations and an adversary relationship.

Yet there is promise. The labor movement and the press are actively discussing the issue of workers' control of pension fund assets and their investment. Such discussion brings increasing recognition of the importance of the role of pension funds in the capital formation process. Further, major unions, as well as the AFL-CIO itself, have committed themselves to the principle of "social investing." The AFL-CIO study and resolution, in fact, goes beyond "social investing" to at least a discussion of the need for pooling of information and assets, and the gathering of information to facilitate workers' exercising their shareholder rights (the depth of the Federation's commitment to this latter effort will be judged by the resources they devote to it). Second, the labor movement is coming to realize that ignoring this issue has cost it dearly, not only in loss of jobs, but in low rates of return, lower than necessary compensation, and (ironically) financing the anti-labor opposition. All this makes it virtually impossible to retreat from at least the more negative forms of control, such as divestiture and boycotting. These may not be the best strategies for control, but they can be effective as educational, propaganda and ideological tactics. Finally, there are a vast number of political allies with whom labor can work in coalition on issues of stock ownership rights and social investing.

One note of caution. In seeking to erode some of the separation between capital ownership and control, one must not forget the vested interests. The financial institutions which currently manage workers' pension fund assets receive four major benefits from that role: commissions, the power to decide terms and conditions of debt, the exercise of ownership rights, and the ability to direct funds to their own investment priorities. Accruing from size and interlocking relationships, these benefits carry with them considerable economic and political power and influence. It is questionable whether such power and influence could have been acquired without the existence of pension fund assets; in any case, pension fund assets now represent a major share of the business of these institutions. One cannot expect them to welcome changes in the institutional arrangements and the focus of power. Gaining control over even a small part of $627 billion of assets is a serious matter. Strategy is important. It is best to begin with a healthy respect for the forces that have established this monopoly control of capital.

The Goals

There are three strategic goals in the campaign for greater control of capital formation. One is to increase the size of workers' assets. The second is to impose workers' investment priorities ("social" or "targeted" investment). The third is to exercise ownership rights.

Increasing the Size of Workers' Assets

Bringing more workers into pension systems and also bargaining for better pension systems will increase workers' assets. But primarily this goal can be reached by exercising management rights allowed by law to raise the rate of return on these assets. If these assets had been growing at a faster rate in the past, the risk of workers never receiving their pensions (because of huge underfunding) would be much less. Even more important, a higher rate of return requires less funding (assuming all other factors hold constant), which means a greater surplus will be available to be bargained into compensation and improvements in working conditions. In addition, there are foreseeable pressures on pension benefit payments—from inflation, from the changes in female work patterns, from pressures on Social Security—which will make a higher return essential if pensions are not to become an increasing proportion of the total compensation package. Finally, a higher rate of return will make more resources available to the pension fund each year, thus enlarging the pool of investable funds available for new investment priorities.

Pursuing this goal will require several combined tactics. First, both collectively bargained and public pension plans must move toward joint administration. The issues of adequate funding, investment policy, and rate of return require it. Clearly, winning joint administration will not be easy; it has not been achieved in most sectors in the past thirty years of bargaining. Hence a second step: unions must educate their workers to understand the importance of the joint administration issue and its relationship to the strategic goals of increasing pension fund assets, social investing, and exercising ownership rights.

Third, the small, segregated pension funds must be pooled together into larger funds which can benefit from modern portfolio theory. The pooling of risk through diversification can significantly increase the rate of return. Increased returns will also come from the economies of information and trading from pooling.

Fourth, a central labor body should create a data bank on the holdings of private and public pension fund assets. Such information is essential for generating strategies that raise the rate of return. In addition, unions can slowly begin to eliminate the middleman costs of transactions. When California teachers are selling shares of stock that Chrysler employees are buying, should each fund pay commissions? Centralization is not difficult with modern technology.

Fifth, union trustees on pension boards must be instructed about asset management. Education should be broad-based, beginning with the role of capital markets and proceeding to the technicalities of the investment instruments available. It should be sophisticated enough to familiarize union people with modern theories of asset management (and the evidence supporting the theory that a fund manager cannot beat the market). The end product of such education is not to remake all trustees into fund managers, but rather to give them the vocabulary and the tools to question those who purport to be making expert statements and expert judgments. Such educational efforts have worked with the range of issues covered by collective bargaining; this task is no more formidable.

Social Investing

Social or targeted investing of pension fund assets generally means going beyond traditional, financial criteria in setting investment priorities. Specifically, it means setting aside a small portion of funds for specific investment projects, giving them priority according to location, capital scarcity, unionization, or social policy—or refusing to invest on many of the same grounds. Much discussion and debate has taken place on this issue.[20]

As indicated in our discussion of pension fund investing and prudence, investment decisions should not be based on purely financial grounds. Yet the ability of pension funds to implement targeted investments is constrained by the likelihood of their effectiveness. For example, public pension funds have been in the vanguard of "social" investing schemes (often on the mistaken assumption that these funds are public money). Much of the demand is for geographic targeting, i.e. investing in Wisconsin businesses or in Massachusetts housing. But given the efficiency of the market in funding profitable investments, such targeting usually means that public pension fund money simply displaces other money, rather than expanding the total amount of capital funding going into these projects.

Various unions have begun to support such schemes, more in principle than in practice. The UAW-Chrysler agreement is a good example of an operative private sector scheme. The UAW does not have a joint trusteeship, but in the 1979 round of bargaining it won a set-aside of 10 percent of pension fund growth. This set-aside will be invested, under the advice of a joint UAW-Chrysler Investment Advisory Committee, in mortgage programs and in nonprofit organizations such as nursing homes, nursery schools, HMOs (Health Maintenance Organizations)—in communities where UAW members live.

In practice, social investing has meant exclusion and divestment, on issues ranging from union-busting and violation of regulations to South Africa. There is a wealth of information available now to make such decisions administratively easy, and the evidence is that the impacts on the portfolio are negligible.[21] Such policies, though, are first and foremost ethical acts. An individual pension fund will have little economic impact on the corporation involved; group action is needed.

Social investing will benefit from all the tactics necessary to increase the size of workers' assets. In addition, there are several tactics uniquely necessary to further social investing. First, a legal strategy must be developed. Although there is legal room to engage in targeted investments, the lines blur when issues of risk and return are not clear-cut. When social investments contain federal guarantees, of course, there is no problem. But those may not be the most interesting or effective schemes. To quote AFSCME's pension counsel:

> The advocate of social investing can develop a clear, pragmatic structural requirement of non-economic criteria in pension investment. . . . Only with careful, specific work, unencumbered by self-interest will the duty of social prudence become the accepted law of pension investments.[22]

Litigation will certainly be necessary, but it is obviously unrealistic to expect an individual labor fiduciary to risk going to jail to establish the limits of social investing. It is better that a central labor body determine what litigation is essential and then back it up with the necessary resources.

Second, pooling set-asides can minimize the risk from social investing. In this way no single pension fund will risk a significant portion of its portfolio and no individual worker's pension will be significantly jeopardized. The AFL-CIO proposal for a reindustrialization fund is in this spirit—clearly patterned after the Scandinavian special funds (without exercise of ownership rights). In reality, several set-aside funds might be necessary, unless agreement can be reached on the priorities of social investing. An obvious target for an independent fund would be a venture-capital fund.

Third, a mechanism must be developed for collective action. This is particularly necessary for divestment and exclusions. Such coordinated acts can be as important to the labor movement as withholding labor power. If used correctly they can affect capital markets and investment by lowering stock values, changing earnings/equity ratios, forcing (unrealized) capital losses on management and other shareholders; and raising the corporation's cost of borrowing.

Exercising Ownership Rights

The importance of exercising control over the board of directors was discussed previously. It represents the ultimate form of control: ownership. But, it will not be easy. If the strategy and tactics already outlined prove successful in increasing the size of workers' assets and raising the return earned on them, the labor movement will almost certainly know the distribution of shares among various pension funds. Then it must monitor the proxy issues and ultimately vote these shares as a group. Perhaps for legal reasons, the unit responsible will only be able to advise how the shares should be voted. But even that is superior to the situation that exists now. The act of simply taking responsibility for voting the shares cannot be underestimated in its impact on corporate and financial management.

Another main tactic is coalition building. A strong movement is already working to democratize corporations, and one of its main concerns is corporate governance.[23] Both outside groups and the SEC (Securities and Exchange Commission) are re-examining proxy rules; they are concerned with taking control of proxy machinery from management and encouraging cumulative voting, which guarantees minority stock-owner representation on the board; creating audit committees, and so forth.[24] Labor should recognize this movement as a valuable ally. Although their respective aims may be ultimately different, the movement for democratic corporate governance has made important gains from which labor can benefit; much can still be done to pursue both groups' aims. In short, an agenda for democratizing the corporation exists. Increased labor interest and input can only aid the goal of democratic control of capital.

Notes

Acknowledgments: I want to thank Randy Barber, Michael Barker, Barry Bluestone, Jocelyn Gutchess, Seamus O'Cleireacain, Buddy Perkel and Dick Prosten for useful and interesting discussions which contributed to this paper. Above all, I am most grateful to District Council 37 AFSCME, Victor Gotbaum, its executive director, and Alan R. Viani, its director of research and negotiations, for providing such a supportive atmosphere in which to do this work.

1. Peter Drucker, *The Unseen Revolution: How Pension Fund Socialism Came to America* (New York: Harper & Row, 1976), p. 1.
2. Editorial, *Pensions and Investments* (7 June 1976), p. 12.
3. "Recent Corporate Financing Patterns," *Federal Reserve Bulletin* 66 (1980): 684.
4. This paragraph draws heavily on Litvak and Daniels (see Selected References).
5. David Vogel, *Lobbying the Corporation* (New York: Basic Books, 1978), p. 95.
6. Adolf A. Berle, Jr., and Gardiner C. Means, *The Modern Corporation and Private Property* (New York: Macmillan Co., 1932).
7. The Congressional Research Service of the Library of Congress compiled an analysis of the fiduciary standards imposed by all the states. See U.S., Congress, House, Committee on Labor and Education, *Pension Task Force Report on Public Employee Retirement Systems* (Washington, D.C.: Government Printing Office, 15 March 1978), pp. 445–471.
8. This estimate is constructed from the numbers in Figure 4-1, as follows:

PERCENT OF ASSETS HAVING EMPLOYEE TRUSTEES

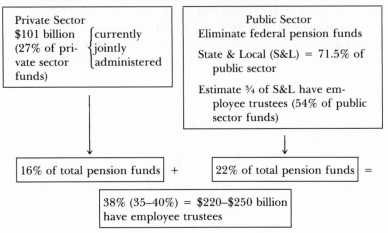

9. See Judith W. Mares, "The Use of Pension Fund Capital: Its Social and Economic Implications—Some Background Issues" (President's Commission on Pension Policy, November 1979), pp. 1–2. The acceptance of pensions as deferred wages stems from *Inland Steel Co.*, 77 NLRB1, enf'd 170 F 2d 247 (CA 7, 1948) *cert. den.*, 336 US 960 (1949).

10. Under ERISA, a corporation going bankrupt is liable for pension fund contributions only up to 30% of its net worth. Many companies which are on shaky financial ground have unfunded liabilities considerably greater than 30% of net worth. According to *Business Week*, in 1979 Lockheed's were 117%, Chrysler's 66%, National Steel's 47%, Bethlehem Steel's 46%. In addition, one should note that this risk might well exceed others stemming from specific investment policies.

11. From a study by A. G. Becker's Fund Evaluation Service, reported in the *Wall Street Journal* (15 April 1980).

12. The S&P index average growth for the decade is taken from the IUD *Pension* Study. The calculation is based on 1970 base assets of $218 billion, growing at 11% annually, with a rate of return differential of 1.6%. The total loss over the decade comes to almost $62 billion, or about $1,000 per worker covered in 1970. Of course, pension fund portfolios consist of more than equities, and the equity component undoubtedly yields a higher rate of return. The S&P index is being used here as a common benchmark, not to imply funds are or should be limited to equity investment.

13. *The Prudence Rule and Pension Plan Investments under ERISA* (U.S. Department of Labor, Labor-Management Services Administration, Pension and Welfare Benefit Programs, 1980), p. 7.

14. Michael T. Leibig, "'You Can't Do That with My Money'—A Search for Mandatory Social Responsibility in Pension Investment," *Journal of Pension Planning and Compliance*, 1980, p. 373.

15. Withers v. Teachers Retirement System of the City of New York, 447 F. Supp. (S.D.N.Y. 1978).

16. *The Prudence Rule*, p. 12.

17. U.S., Congress, Senate, Committee on Governmental Affairs, Subcommittee on Reports, Accounting and Finances, *Voting*

Rights in Major Corporations (Washington, D.C.: Government Printing Office, January 1978).
18. Harold E. Bigler, "Statement before the President's Commission on Pension Policy," (10 December 1979), pp. 4–5.
19. This is a different issue from the "Meidner Plan," which focuses on using excess profits that result from the trade union wage policy of solidarity helping lower-paid workers to fund workers' ownership. See Rudolf Meidner, *Employee Investment Funds* (London: George Allen & Unwin, 1978).
20. Mares, "Pension Fund Capital," provides a useful summary of the issues and the literature.
21. One reason why exclusion does not lower the rate of return on the entire portfolio is that the standard economic criteria exclude whole classes of investment from the portfolio. For evidence on portfolio effects see Stuart Baldwin et al., *Pension Funds and Ethical Investment: A Study of Investment Practice and Opportunities, State of California Retirement Systems* (New York: Council on Economic Priorities, 1980).
22. Leibig, p. 394.
23. Vogel offers an excellent discussion of this movement.
24. The Council on Economic Priorities publishes an annual review and progress report on such issues. See, for example, Steven D. Lydenberg, *Minding the Corporate Conscience, 1980* (New York: Council on Economic Priorities, 1980).

Selected References

Abuse on Wall Street: Conflicts of Interest in the Securities Market. The Twentieth Century Fund, 1980.
AFL-CIO Pension Fund Study. Washington, D.C.: AFL-CIO, 1980.
Coltman, E., and Metzenbaum, S. *Investing in Ourselves: Strategies for Massachusetts.* Massachusetts Social and Economic Opportunity Council, June 1979.
Leibig, Michael T. " 'You Can't Do That with My Money'—A Search for Mandatory Social Responsibility in Pension Investment," *Journal of Pension Planning and Compliance*, 1980.
Litvak, Lawrence, and Daniels, Belden. *Innovations in Development Finance.* Washington, D.C.: Council of State Planning Agencies, 1979.

Mares, Judith W. *The Use of Pension Fund Capital: Its Social and Economic Implications—Some Background Issues.* Working Paper, President's Commission on Pension Policy.

Pensions: A Study of Benefit Fund Investment. Industrial Union Department, AFL-CIO, May 28, 1980.

Rifkin, J., and Barber, R. *The North Shall Rise Again.* Boston: Beacon Press, 1978.

PART II

Industrial Dislocation and Structural Change

5

Industrial Dislocation in Europe

EDITH CRESSON

Edith Cresson is an economist and long-time leading member of the French Socialist party. During 1979–81 she served as a deputy to the European parliament. Madame Cresson is currently the minister of agriculture in the new French socialist government.

The recent change of regime in France renders her paper all the more pertinent. She analyzes industrial dislocation throughout Western Europe, the individual national responses to the post-1973 economic crisis, and the lack of a common European industrial policy. She then reviews the successes and limitations of existing (postwar) social democratic economic policies and concludes with a strong case for industrial policies proposed by the French socialists—policies which, since her writing, are in the process of being implemented.

INDUSTRIAL DISLOCATION IN EUROPE

Edith Cresson

Industrial Dislocation: A Description

From 1960 to 1973, European countries with the exception of the United Kingdom experienced fast and steady industrial growth. Their economies were thus able to harmonize production structures, and European multinational companies invested outside Europe, especially in the United States.

That situation has changed. Industrial dislocation now afflicts all these countries in at least three forms: a relative contraction in industrial employment, a relative contraction in industrial production (in current prices or in volume), and a lasting balance of trade deficit (the inability to compensate for imports with a sufficient level of exports).

Let us begin with employment. Statistics show a considerable decline after 1970 in industrial employment as a percentage of the total employment in all the EEC countries.

This loss of jobs in the industrial sector was not compensated by an increase in the other sectors. Indeed, from 1973 to 1977 the EEC lost approximately 1,170,000 jobs, while the United States 9,933,000 and Japan 1,631,000. In France, the tertiary (or service) sector was responsible for the creation of three new jobs out of four between 1962 and 1977. But now computers in the

77

tertiary sector will considerably reduce the possibilities of employment. Banking and insurance activities, for instance, forecast a reduction of 30 percent in the coming decade.

Between 1979 and 1980, the total number of Western Europeans on unemployment compensation increased by 20 percent (50 percent in the United Kingdom) and the percentage of unemployed people under twenty-five years old keeps growing (the percentage was 41.4 percent in the EEC in October 1980).

Let us examine the main features of European industry prior to and then after the key years of 1967–73.

From 1960 on, the existence of the Common Market motivated firms to adapt and to increase trade inside the EEC. None of the EEC countries deprived itself of the fundamental sectors. Italy and Holland built up a steel industry, France and Belgium a capital goods industry, Germany a powerful food industry. Sectors with a high growth rate (the automobile industry, non-coal energy, chemicals, electric and electronic materials) and sectors in decline (coal, textile, clothing, agricultural products) were mainly the same in each of the EEC countries. Although European industrial groups were scarce (Agfa-Gevaert, Dunlop-Pirelli), national groups of an international size had been built up through concentration. The phenomenon of multinational companies was no longer limited to the United States. In 1960, 100 of the 160 most important firms in the main industrial sectors were American. By 1970 the number had dropped to sixty. Of course there are wide variations in the industrial sectors. For instance, although the United Kingdom could boast only a middling performance, it possessed the five top-ranking food companies of the EEC, and the profits of the ICI (Imperial Chemical, the fifth chemical firm of the EEC) were higher than those of the three most important German chemical groups.

Lately these large European groups have invested abroad, especially in the United States. This increase of investments has speeded up productivity in France, Germany, Italy and, to a lesser extent the United Kingdom, much more than in the United States. Compare the figures in Table 5-1. Only Japan surpassed the European results. The investment effort was made easier by the divergent evolution of capital and labor costs, especially in the capital goods sector. From 1960 to 1973, investment costs in capital goods and wage costs followed this pattern (see Table 5-2).

As Table 5-2 indicates, it became cheaper for employers in

TABLE 5-1
INCREASE OF THE WORK PRODUCTIVITY
PER HOUR IN THE INDUSTRIAL FIELD
(growth rates in %)

	Period	Total economic activity	Manufacturing industry
Germany	1961–68	+4.9%	+5.9%
	1969–73	5.3	5.0
	1974–78	4.0	4.0
France	1961–70	4.9	5.8
	1971–73	5.7	5.5
	1974–78	4.0	4.9
Italy	1959–68	7.1	7.3
	1969–73	6.2	7.1
	1974–77	2.5	2.6
U.K.	1959–68	3.2	4.4
	1969–73	3.2	3.3
	1974–78	1.0	0.0 ('74–'77)
U.S.A.	1956–65	3.1	2.9
	1966–73	2.3	2.4
	1974–78	0.8	1.6

From: U.S.A. : Private business sector
       Germany : Gesanite Wirkschaeft
       France : Branches activités non-agricoles
       U.K.   : Global economy Gross Domestic
                 Product per employee hour
       Source: E.E.C. Commission.

the 1960s to invest in machines than in labor intensive production. Thus from 1960 to 1973, new jobs were scarce if not non-existent. The employment level in 1973 was only marginally higher than in 1960 (31.7 million jobs instead of 31.1).

After the key years of 1970–73, industrial employment started to decrease even in the most dynamic fields, such as chemicals. This evolution occurred in 1967–69 in most EEC countries, though France and Belgium experienced a slight increase in industrial employment. The United Kingdom registered a decline in each of its industrial branches (except energy and chemicals). The same evolution occurred in the United States and in European countries outside the EEC. Italy, Ireland, Spain, Portugal, Greece and Japan registered the same evolution, but somewhat later, in 1972–73.

TABLE 5-2
INDUSTRIAL COSTS IN 1973
(base year 1960 = 100)

	Investment costs in capital goods	Pay cost per unit of work produced
Germany	138	180
France	150	184
Italy	168	209
U.K.	170	197
Holland	153	238

The European countries dealt with the post-1973 crisis in different ways. On the whole, Germany and Holland adapted by reducing costs and industrial employment. The restructuring has taken place by a decrease in labor-intensive industries and has stimulated capital goods industries. These countries have reached a high growth rate in their industrial exports, which was made easier by a devaluation of their currency.

The United Kingdom and Italy adapted by accepting a drop in their labor productivity and a lower growth rate in industrial exports. France and Belgium entered the crisis later. Electoral considerations in France have slowed down restructuring, especially in the steel industry, and have exacerbated the situation.

In spite of these differences, a general phenomenon has appeared: persistent low levels of industrial investments (compensated in France in large part by big national companies which accounted for 25 percent productive investment in 1978). These low levels do not result from the financial situation of firms but from lowered demand. This is alarming, especially considering the new investments taking place in the Third World while European plants grow older.

These responses to the post-1973 crisis have brought different results. German industry retains its dominant position. It has continued the reorientation process begun in 1960, but at a price of one million jobs since 1974. Meanwhile, it continued its emphasis on research and development, and German investment in capital goods increased in 1978–79 by 15 percent (in France by 3 percent).

French industry continues its belated effort of restructuring. The absence of controls on industrial prices has raised profits. However, continuing pay discrimination, income differentials, and the absence of any social consensus make it impossible to import the German model into France, as we shall see later.

Italy is the only country which continued to create industrial jobs from 1973 to 1977. At the same time, it developed an underground economy, with people taking two or three jobs in the commercial and technological sectors where wages remain extremely low.

In the United Kingdom the drop in productivity has not prevented the economy from losing 500,000 jobs since 1973. New possibilities opened up by oil revenues have not resulted in a modernization of national industries.

These diverse experiences have altered the industrial situation in Europe. The European countries occupy a generally less favorable position than the United States and Japan, but they also occupy different levels in each industrial sector. Hence they are unable to consider a joint industrial policy similar to their joint agricultural policy. For instance, in the areas facing strong competition from underdeveloped countries (textiles, shoes, electronic components), Germany is the only country that has phased out such production. France and Belgium are slowly withdrawing, but Italy and Great Britain continue to compete. In areas involving high levels of skilled work (mechanical industry, professional electronics), the position of the EEC countries is far better, and they continue to export (especially Germany). Japan doubled its share of the computers and telecommunications market from 1963 to 1975, at the expense of the United States and the United Kingdom. But Germany is still in a good position, and France and Italy are making progress in this crucial area. To sum up, Germany has quickly adapted to the trends of the international division of labor. The other countries have adapted also, but less effectively.

Probably the two most promising fields for the future are information technology and energy innovation. The EEC enjoys a good position in the automation market (behind Japan but in front of the United States) and in working out the use of microprocessors, especially in mechanical industries. National policies on energy differ widely. The stress in France is on nuclear energy; there is an insufficient effort to conserve energy. Nuclear safety is in any case a divisive issue in the European parliament.

Some industrial sectors have become the subject of EEC regulatory agreements, such as the naval industry (where

Japanese competition, which accounts for 80 percent of all contracts, is considerable), chemical fibers and textiles. The steel industry probably possesses the best of these agreements. Clause 52 of the European Coal and Steel Community, which regulates production by an agreement between the members of the EEC, has recently been applied for the first time. This measure became necessary after a drop in the market price and a decline in demand.

What is striking about this joint industrial policy—still in embryo—is its defensive character and the fact that it mainly protects sectors in decline (despite a few successes, such as Airbus, Eurodif, Ariane). But the essential problems lie within the classical sectors: the automobile industry, chemicals, mechanical industry, and electrical appliances. These sectors need two weapons: the technological ability to innovate, and a market share sufficient to enable the reduction of costs by large-scale production. A merely national framework is too limited. A European reconstruction has begun, but it too is still limited—to Pilkington and St. Gobain in the glass industry, Michelin and Dunlop-Pirelli in the tire industry, and Nestlé and Unilever in the food industry. Some cooperation is likely in the automobile industry. However, faced with Japanese penetration, some industrial managers prefer to work out agreements with Japanese firms (Nissan-Alfa Romeo; Honda-British Leyland) rather than deal with European production conditions (wages, work conditions, and so forth). It is also true that the Germans, because of their great industrial strength, are reticent about joining an integrated industrial policy.

Causes of Industrial Dislocation

At least four causes underlie the industrial dislocation currently afflicting Europe: the world-wide growth of the economy, energy costs, the growth rate in household consumption, and political factors. The four are interdependent and reinforce each other. To compensate for the rise in energy prices, for example, every country must export, and to export they must price their products competitively. Thus they have to engage in large-scale production to recover or defend their domestic market.

On the other hand, there is a joint responsibility between industrial countries. When trade increases, everyone tries to take advantage of the situation. In this economic warfare, which sometimes has positive benefits, points are scored by those who have power over prices, the investment process, and the signing of contracts. Therefore multinational companies engage in more and more diversified activities. This pattern, which is world-wide, most affects semi-finished products (steel and chemical products, for example).

When world demand is stagnant, production in the concerned sectors contracts, the unit costs increase, and finally investments decrease. Sometimes this leaves production in those sectors solely to rival countries. The effect may be less extreme, but when firms are obliged to accept the international price as a given, the increase in their costs produces a contraction in their production and a reduction of the margins. This in turn limits the firm's ability to open up new channels for trade and research.

The situation of firms in sectors that benefit from international demand is quite different. Their wage costs can be added to prices without the loss of the firm's competitive position.

The growing competitiveness of Third World countries reveals itself in a deterioration of the balance of trade—in other words, a reduction in exports and an increase in imports. From 1970 to 1977, the exports of the nine EEC countries, compared to world exports, varied from 17.8 percent to 25.8 percent.

It is noteworthy that Germany (see Table 5-3) has improved its position in spite of the rise in its unit costs, thanks to an orientation towards markets with a high growth rate. In fact, 47 percent of German exports come from leading industries where the pressure on prices is less strong.

TABLE 5-3
NATIONAL SHARES OF TOTAL WORLD
EXPORT TRADE (in %)

	1950	1960	1970	1977
U.K.	25.5	16.5	10.8	9.3
France	9.9	9.6	8.7	9.9
Germany	7.3	19.3	19.8	20.8
Japan	3.4	6.9	11.7	15.4
U.S.A.	27.3	21.6	18.5	15.9

The ability of the industrial structures in Europe to adapt to foreign and domestic demands requires an analysis of the policies affecting quality and reliability—that is to say, of non-price characteristics which ensure a strong position on expanding markets. Product quality and reliability are perhaps as important as price in their effect on export sales. Japan leads in this area. Fujitsu has been selling more computers in Japan than IBM this year, and will export 30 percent of its production with Hitachi and Nippon Electric. The Japanese export three-fourths of their machine tools and increased their sales to Germany by 80 percent in 1979. The five world leaders in the hi-fi market are Japanese, as are three-fourths of the world's most expensive cameras. Sony and Matsushita control 88 percent of the magnetoscope market in Germany, 95 percent in France, and 100 percent in America. The Japanese cover one-third of the steel needs of California, and are making advances in microbiology which will allow them to dominate the food sector.

The authorities have difficulty responding to such challenges, thanks in part to the complexity of a situation in which technological characteristics, types of markets and changing strategical situations are all factors.

Probably the two countries in the world best able to respond to the dislocation crisis are Germany and Japan. Though they have very different social systems, the two countries share a common characteristic: a vital and ongoing social dialogue between business and labor. It seems that in addition to technological potential and the will to conquer markets, this factor plays an important role. I shall return to it during my discussion of the socialist proposals.

First, however, let us consider the economic crisis in France in more detail. Since 1970, when only 200,000 French workers were unemployed, the situation has grown steadily worse—one million in 1977, 1.3 million in 1979, and 1.4 million in 1980. All the forecasts predict a doubling of the 1980 figure by 1985.

The French economy is characterized by many negative factors. Concentration favors traditional noncompetitive practices which go unpenalized. Costs of production are high, not so much from wages as from the rigidity of management (the proportion of white-collar workers is higher than in Germany) and the inegalitarian character of the society (one worker out of two earns less than $750 per month). Useless costs are prevalent, such as superfluous expenditures whose aim is to stress French "glamor" or to raise the income of the ruling classes (cars, official residences, unnecessary staff and so on). Half of the French industrial firms are under minority family control, a situation which seldom produces a positive bookkeeping profit, so costs are overloaded. Then too there are high handling costs—the distribution network is marked by a levy on profits. This amplifies the inflation rate and recent government policies of price decontrol have amplified it further. There are also many social costs (waste, lost time and so forth). Further, the proportion of the gross domestic product assigned to research and development is much smaller than in the United States, the German Federal Republic, the United Kingdom and Japan. Coupled with an insufficient development of exports, there is a decreasing domestic market (15 percent of the domestic market was lost in ten years, 5 percent since 1973). Thus there is a dependency, especially for investment goods. We know that the control of the domestic market is a preliminary to any rise in exporting capacity and thus is a *sine qua non* of competitiveness. (In 1979, manufactured goods represented 97 percent of the Japanese exports and 26 percent of their imports in comparison with 77 percent and 60 percent in France.) Finally, France suffers from the absence of any social dialogue (particularly damaging, for instance, in the steel industry).

The Social Democratic Response

The social democratic experiences of Western Europe are founded on a double compromise—between capital and labor and between the state and the market. This double compromise will work only if it is founded on a balance of power which favors the workers and their organizations vis-à-vis capital, and favors the socialist party vis-à-vis political formations of the center and right.

Western European social democratic experiences traditionally have been based on the development of collective services and corresponding investments (housing, health, education), global encouragement of investment or a government role in the investment process, and more direct economic intervention—national investment firms, nationalizations, creation of public firms. Still, these efficient systems followed "mixed economy" policies.

First, there is labor market policy. In the short term, it rests on a successful proportioning of fiscal, budget and monetary policies and also on an implicit incomes policy. Business and labor agree on an increase in wages and wage costs. (From time to time this comes about as a result of an extended strike.) Usually this social partnership takes place in a situation of modern, efficient capitalism. When this is not the case, as in the United Kingdom, the policy tends to fail. Labor market policy, which is essential for productivity and competitiveness, results from a balance between economic and social constraints. For workers this means not only a lessening of inequalities, but the possibility to influence the operation of the labor market and to express their opinion about the organization of labor itself. This is usually done through a joint, tripartite (labor, business, government) management of employment policy.

Welfare policies aim at constructing a more tolerable society for the weak and expecting more from the strong. A partial levelling of incomes is accomplished through fiscal policy and income transfers, wider social protection, and reforms in education.

Finally, there are policies concerned with forwarding economic democracy; these have increased in number and importance since the mid-1960s. Some offer greater powers to joint management committees, as in Germany and Holland; the Swedish contractual model emphasizes collective bargaining; in others we find increased participation of trade unions at all levels of decision-making, as in Austria.

Despite these postwar gains, the social democratic movement is undergoing setbacks. Capitalists have succeeded in stemming the trend toward economic democracy. The current crisis with its high levels of unemployment has clearly tilted the balance of power to the side of employers. Social democrats, now on the defensive, must ponder the following questions: Is there any additional compromise possible between the state and the market? That is to say, between further socialization of income and consumption and capitalist domination of the productive process? And how can socialists formulate policies that take new social values into account, such as the status of women and young people and matters of ecology?

Whatever their new policies, socialists must retain their traditional priorities: a return to full employment, a minimum set of social guarantees for all, and improvement in all aspects of work life. Prospective socialist policies will concentrate on the following areas:

- A new development model, which includes optimal use of new technologies, greater decentralization, access to information, more time off, division of labor, more and better public space and housing;
- A more direct role of the state in determining supply (nationalization, research, incentives, and so forth);
- Reintegrating disaffected groups and classes through improved social welfare and through employment programs involving government, management, and labor;
- The strengthening of economic democracy, and in particular dealing with the special problems presented by a computerized society;
- A struggle against inflation both through compromise with business and by state intervention.

The French Case

State intervention is a French tradition. It is not unique to social democrats, since right-wing governments have long followed such a policy. Yet despite excessive intervention and centralization, the present French government follows laissez-faire policies when it comes to profits, conglomerates, inherited incomes, protection of the domestic market, and rampant tax evasion.

In addition, French society is characterized by an absence of any social dialogue and by a Communist party supported by some 20 percent of the electorate. Over the period from 1971 to 1980, the socialist party gradually surpassed the Communist party in electoral importance. But the communists seemed to have preferred maintaining the right wing in power to playing a secondary role to the socialists. This has created in France an explosive—but at the same time paralyzing—situation. It encourages the right wing to believe that it can deal with the current economic crisis on its own terms—and at the expense of previous social gains and (if necessary) of basic liberties. French socialists know that any answer to the policy of the right wing is impossible without the union of all popular forces. They count on the communist electorate, which for the first time in history seems to understand and to reject the policy of the government.

French socialists know that social democratization similar to the German or Scandinavian models would improve the situation of workers in France. However, they are intent on proposing policies specifically appropriate to France. They start with this premise: the liberal system, far from correcting the inadequacies of the French economy, reinforces them. Since it does not take into account or adjust to changes in French industry, it leaves itself wholly dependent on multinational capitalism.

French industrial policy since 1970 has brought disastrous results hidden by some successes. The increase in exports temporarily obscures the ever-decreasing French share of the domestic market. We know that there can be no share in the world market (which is essential to large-scale production, hence to lower costs) without a successful market at home. But rather than invest in a shrinking domestic market, entrepreneurs reduce their staff, consequently narrowing export possibilities. In this way loss of the domestic market leads to a decrease in the share of foreign markets, to unemployment, and to a worsening of the balance of trade deficit.

Profits are indeed amassed from the policy of freeing prices, but they are not invested in industry, but rather in speculative fields. And so authorities have gradually lost control over production. France exports raw materials (leather, wool, agricultural products) which then return as manufactured products. Worse, no measures have been taken to ensure that the technological revolution (in data processing, for example) will prove favorable to the French economy.

The Giscard Government's liberal policy tolerates an outmoded distribution system, special privileges, inherited incomes, tax evasions, and so on. Supporters of the government defend this combination of corruption and incompetence in the name of "liberty." Meanwhile the government does nothing to stop the decline in the manufacture of investment goods. It favors inequalities which produce inflation, counts on unemployment to control social unrest, and accepts the total domination of the French economy by multinational companies. The government proposes no industrial policy at the European level.

Socialists recognize that an overall industrial policy is essential. As we have seen, it is illusory to count on the tertiary sector or the administration (despite the need to improve some sectors, such as education and health) to create new jobs to offset those lost in the current process of government-encouraged industrial dislocation. At the same time, French socialists refuse to accept an international division of labor in which some goods are manufactured in recently-developed countries whose labor costs are less expensive. It is not that these products (shoes, clothing, electronic hardware) can be manufactured efficiently only in other countries, but that French manufacturing is out of date and uncompetitive. We must search for the lowest manufacturing costs, even for goods manufactured in newly industrialized countries. Such a policy creates jobs not only in the manufacturing fields, but also in the leading industries. It is not necessary to manufacture everything, providing we regain some of the ground so carelessly abandoned. The mastering of new techniques (data processing, telecommunications) is also essential, since it will lead to a rigorous investment policy and hence a share of the industrial market in fields which are future-oriented.

Socialists see nationalizations neither as penalties nor solutions for companies and sectors in difficulty. On the contrary, socialists propose to nationalize, with selectivity and moderation, the most promising industries. The right wing nationalizes only after a bankruptcy, when it is already too late. The prime example is the French steel industry, which has become the subject of a creeping nationalization. The point of nationalizing the leading industries is precisely to break corporate domination.

Speed is an essential factor in the industrial process. He who wins is he who is first to master a technique. In France, machine-tools industries, agricultural motor industries, and data-processing industries are hard to find. New technologies (biology, renewable energies, data processing) must be applied quickly and under favorable conditions.

The building of a modern industrial sector requires a plan which is democratically discussed by the social actors. The plan must encompass investment decisions, the signing of contracts, public-oriented research incentives, and industrial reconversions. There must be a nationalization of credit to reorient investments. At present, 90 percent of credit comes from private banks, and has led to speculative rather than productive investments. The recovery of the domestic market, which is vital to employment, to exports, and to national independence, depends on these measures. And clearly, there also must be more dialogue between social partners. French employers, after all, did not officially recognize trade unions until 1968. In fact, social relations in France are getting worse, unlike the case in most social democracies. Our socialist proposals would initially favor both capital and labor, for the situation of the economy is rapidly deteriorating. Later on, our aim as socialists would be to shift the balance of power to labor.

French socialists would stress education and a continuing training policy to teach workers new techniques; we would encourage research and work to reduce working hours and the hierarchy of incomes. All these are necessary not only for social justice, but because the new industrial revolution requires significant participation by workers in the organization of work, including its decision-making processes. Again, France is extremely late in this field compared with the Western European social democracies.

In addition, French socialists would propose a policy of social protection in which the employers' contribution stems from cash flow or the values added. Employers' contributions based on wages penalizes labor-intensive firms and limits employment.

Finally, a socialist industrial policy must take into account aid for developing countries. Often the low-cost prices in these countries result from an operating policy which profits multinational companies that stop investing in Europe. Thus it is suitable to connect foreign aid to the observation of the standards of the International Labor Office (ILO) (as Mr. Cheysson wished during the Lomé Convention) and to control the practices of multinational companies on the European level. Second, this aid should extend local potential rather than create artificial activities that upset existing social structures. Third, the aid should be based on a study of the employment possibilities as foreseen in the report "A New World Employment Plan," proposed by the Confederation of Socialist Parties of the EEC. These proposals are the basis of what the French socialists call "social growth."

6

New Technology and Its Impact on the Work Force

ULRICH STEGER

Ulrich Steger is a Social Democratic Party (SPD) member of the German Parliament. An economist and former professor, he is vice-chair of the SPD Parliamentary Working Council.

Steger addresses the economic and social problems posed by new technologies, particularly microelectronics. He argues that to avoid disruptive structural changes, the State must make investment decisions that utilize these new technologies to fulfill social needs (in the fields of housing, energy, transportation, and work environment, for example) and at the same time to ensure full employment. Above all, the workers themselves, through their trade unions, must be involved at all levels of economic decision-making.

NEW TECHNOLOGY AND ITS IMPACT ON THE WORK FORCE

Ulrich Steger

Any survey of the past soon reveals the enormous extent to which technological development has influenced the world in which we live and work. The conurbation, the car, television and the assembly line are hallmarks of the twentieth century.

A serious effort to analyse the future can only give rise to serious doubts about the all-embracing influence of technology. The technologies of tomorrow are today only potential, possible technologies whose realization depends partly on changeable factors such as economics and politics. This does not mean, however, that development can be shaped according to desire. Technology possesses a considerable inertia that resists control or guidance. On closer inspection, the relevant parameters for a forecast are numerous, their relationships very complex. In such a complex system cause and effect can easily change places.

In this article the relationships between labor and technology must be treated in a more simplified manner. The first part gives a short historical resume and briefly debates the theory of long waves in techological innovation, because there are really several empirical bases for it today. In the following discussion of the basic technologies most important for the future—raw materials, energy and materials technology, microelectronics and biotechnology—the emphasis is on the possibilities for applying the new technologies.

The complexity of the subject makes it impossible to discuss the potential social changes the new technologies might create; consideration is given only to the effect on labor. Extrapolating from current economic problems, which have already led to high levels of unemployment in the industrialized nations, the paper develops the following arguments:

- the economic crisis in the industrialized nations, which is caused primarily by internal factors, is essentially a disproportion between production and productivity growth rates;
- the technologies of tomorrow will allow a return to full employment and make it possible to overcome "growth limits"— but they could just as easily lead to even higher unemployment levels;
- the economic policy adopted by the State is a major determinant of the future;
- a purely "neoclassical" strategy will lead to higher unemployment and benefit technologies intended to improve cost-effectiveness;
- a mixture of tactics orientated around supply and demand is an alternative which will guarantee jobs (modernization policy);
- the qualitative as well as quantitative effects of new technologies require particular attention. In particular, the effects which microelectronics are having on the labor situation prove the importance of "making working life more humane" for workers.

Main Trends of Technological Development

Technology and Society in the Twentieth Century

Economic history reveals that the application (but not the development) of new technologies takes place in fits and starts. It follows that innovations in products and processes are closely related. The car, for example, would never have acquired its supreme economic and social significance without the innovative assembly line process. Had car production remained purely a craft, the purchasing power of the public during the 1940s could never have created a mass demand. This is why many people consider the introduction of assembly line production to be Ford's major innovation; only in this way could costs be sufficiently reduced for mass demand to develop.[1]

This example also suggests the lasting effect of technology on living and working conditions. Although the monotony of the assembly line (which dominates far more than car production) increased man's alienation from his work, thus creating a greater need for means of relieving mental tension, for leisure, living in the open country, and so forth, the car proved the means with which to satisfy this need. But there were other negative effects, including urban sprawl, despoliation of the countryside as a result of ever more roads, traffic chaos in the towns, and the decline of public transport.

The car industry is not unique. Many of the technologies responsible for production and growth today were developed in the forties and applied in the fifties and sixties. Other technologies which developed in this period of much innovation include: major blast furnace systems, the Linz-Donawitz process, continuous casting, rolling mill automation, mass production of special steel; chemical engineering, plastics, synthetic fibres, detergents, dyes, pharmaceuticals; electrical consumer goods (and related services in radio and television, film and other media); and aircraft and missile technology.

These dynamic technologies, with their initially latent but great development potential, also came to involve other branches of industry; they stimulated improvements and innovations in (among others) mechanical engineering, transport and traffic, energy technology, and construction.[2]

In retrospect, our modern society with its general prosperity appears as the inevitable consequence of these technologies. Equally inevitably, production processes with high capital investment reduce the worker to fulfilling subsidiary functions in the production process, alienate him from the actual content of his work and arouse a need for satisfaction in leisure and excessive consumption. On the other hand, mass production and the economics of scale make it possible to satisfy these newly awakened needs. The availability of labor-saving domestic appliances and pseudo-communication through the media have made possible the small, mobile families essential for modern production processes, but also to a large extent cut off communication—communication with potentially serious political consequences—among the workers themselves. On the other hand, the relatively stable "social peace" resulting from this social stupor in most of the industrialised nations has helped democratic institutions to function and made it possible for them to rectify cases where development has gone seriously wrong. The higher tax revenues required for these purposes were easily acquired, since the new technologies and economic structures also led to higher productivity and income levels in the second half of the century.

Key Technologies of the Future[3]

The fragility of the modern mass consumer society and the welfare state is currently being analysed from many sides. One powerful force for change already exists. New technologies have been developed in recent years which already have considerable economic potential and could soon reshape society, although this potential is to a large extent still latent today. The most important basic innovations are in microelectronics, atomic energy, solar energy, biotechnology, and new materials technologies.

Technical Developments in Electronics

Electronics is a basic technology which will have a decisive influence on the development of almost all other technologies. Only by using electronics is it economically feasible to store large quantities of alphanumerical and graphic data (memory technology), to process them (integrated circuits, microprocessors, etc.) and to input or output them in written, printed or verbal form, or in the form of electrical control signals (peripherals technology). Microelectronics thus makes a decisive contribution towards transforming the relationship between man and machine into a relationship between machine and machine, thereby ensuring complete automatization of all processes.

The development of highly integrated chips with hundreds of thousands of logic functions will lead to substantial changes in production and business offices—at least they will when memory and software developments and sensor technology, which at present still lag behind, catch up or at least reach a more advanced stage. Above all, there will be substantial changes in production technology (mechanical engineering) and in office technology. Microelectronics thus affect a majority of all jobs and, therefore, working conditions (see p. 107).

Robot Technology

Robots or automatons will acquire a dominant position in production processes once they have been equipped with artificial intelligence (these are called third-generation robots). Robot systems will be used almost everywhere where there are iterative work processes; where the volume of work is sufficient to make technical solutions economically feasible; where it is basically a case of handling objects and not of dealing with people; and where the work is unpleasant, unsocial, dangerous, or impossible for man.

They can be used in a wide range of activities, including assembly of parts and structural components, handling workpieces, welding, and varnishing. These activities, which still require very high expenditure in wages, will almost certainly become increasingly automated in the future.

Automation in Offices

Almost half the entire working population in the Federal Republic of Germany is employed in offices and in administration. Technological changes will therefore have a particularly strong effect on office and administrative professions. They have already begun: at first all the production spheres of a company will be integrated in terms of information technology (the fully electronic office), and then (or even at the same time) there will be supra-regional integration (electronic mail).

The introduction of modern information technologies will have a double effect: an increased ability to process information on the one hand, and a decreasing mechanical work output for personnel on the other. Despite this shift, however, we can expect an increase from 10 million to 11.8 million in office and administration personnel by 1990.

In the longer term, the further development of "electronic intelligence" will allow intelligent (technical, cost-efficient) decision-making to be taken over by machine. "Electronic servants" in private households will likely follow.

The technology that will affect the working environment most is microelectronics. On the other hand, its development is also very flexible and will respond to changing values, attitudes, and organizational forms in society. Catch-phrases such as "the automated society" or "the information society," therefore, should not be accepted blindly as prophecies of an inevitable future. Unfortunately, it is doubtful that microelectronics will make work easier or lead to large reductions in working hours, as many people expect, and there is also the danger that even greater dependence on machines will lead to mass unemployment.

Energy Technology

The availability of cheap energy is an issue of major importance for every industrial system. The ways and means, as well as the cost of supplying the energy, influence the production system, consumption, and the level of social prosperity. Until the end of the century, fossil energy (oil, coal, natural gas) will continue as before to be the dominant energy form, but will burden all industrial economies with considerably higher costs. Since for technical reasons alone the energy alternatives (atomic and solar energy) can scarcely be of great import before the turn of the century, the traditional energy system will be a major factor affecting working and living conditions.

The need to save fossil fuel will probably encourage decentralization in some industries; it is already apparent that a combination of heat pumps, insulation, district heating can lower energy costs in some areas. Pressure towards increasing productivity will also encourage progress in technologies that require less capital expenditure, such as microelectronics. The drive to conserve may also favor new forms of building and living arrangements that will meet the aims of the "alternative movement" better than they do today.

Since relatively more will have to be spent on basic needs (housing, energy, food), we can expect a slower rise in "freely" expendable private income. In the long term this can lead to changes in consumer attitudes and living habits, to a longer service life of consumer goods and more careful and economical treatment of them.

Raw Materials and Materials Technology

A scarcity or rise in the price of raw materials could also have a braking effect on industrial development, but despite currently rising prices, a general scarcity is hardly to be expected. Substitute materials and processes are already beginning to appear on the market. In addition, process technologies and robot systems are opening new possibilities for recycling raw materials.

One main change in materials technology could take place if sufficient quantities of carbon fibers come on the market at low prices. Carbon fibers have the following advantages over metals: corrosion resistance, lower weight, scuff resistance, and greater stability. Especially in conjunction with electronics, these new materials can make a considerable contribution to the revolution in production technology and product design. Equally important, electronics (automation) makes it possible to manufacture these materials automatically and, therefore, at greatly reduced cost.

Biotechnology

Many scientists believe that biotechnology and its auxiliary sciences, especially microbiology, will acquire an importance in the near future comparable to that of microelectronics. The aim of all biotechnical processes is to use metabolic-physiological and biochemical processes in biological systems for technical purposes, especially for production. In this respect, suitable biological systems are primarily micro-organisms such as bacteria, yeasts and other fungi, sometimes unicellular algae and the cells or tissue of higher plants and animals and, finally, certain cell-free enzymes isolated from these organisms. The potential for synthesis of those organisms can be used to create technically useful products or to convert certain substances into others. The range of biosynthetic and intermediate products is very wide and includes basic foodstuffs and additives (protein, amino acids), basic pharmaceuticals (antibiotics), substances not detrimental to the environment (citric acid, biological insecticides) and raw materials (metals, ethanol).

Biotechnology already enjoys a long tradition. For centuries man has tried, at first purely empirically, later using scientific methods, to heighten biological processes by using technological principles. A considerable number of processes were developed in this way, such as fermentation, which is still used today in dairy farming, breweries and distilleries.

In the last twenty years, however, the biological auxiliary sciences of biotechnology have undergone a far-reaching transformation from primarily descriptive disciplines into experimental disciplines. The center of attention here is the comprehensive analysis of life processes using molecular-biological, chemical and physical methods of analysis. This breakthrough of research into the cell and molecular biological functions has led to a deepened understanding of these processes. On the basis of this new knowledge, biotechnology is being applied to new areas; these range from unconventional food technology to environmental protection technology and special sections of pharmaceutical technology and even to raw materials technology. Biotechnology will clearly play an outstanding role in further industrial-economic development. It has the potential to reduce wastes while considerably extending the supply of food and raw materials.

Technology and Labor in a Mixed Economy

In an economic system which measures economic success in terms of capital yields, paid labor is a special cost factor for the individual company. Whereas capital investment normally pays itself back through yields (depreciation) and thus allows the company to retain control of the funds invested, wages paid are irrevocably removed from the control of the individual company. This is the most powerful incentive for replacing labor with capital, and the decisive instrument with which to accomplish it is technology.

Neoclassical economists (monetarists) question the necessity of replacing labor with capital by arguing that the wage rate, or the cost of labor is the decisive factor. The lower the cost of labor (the lower the wages demanded in the face of threatened unemployment), the lower the compulsion to replace labor with capital. Here, however, the interdependence of the parties—sometimes called the "closed (business) cycle"—comes into play. Time and again Marx and Keynes argued this point most convincingly. At a given historical stage of economic and social development, a neoclassical strategy of reducing wages or, as in the past, simply permitting the "invisible hand" of the market forces to work, does *not* compel companies to return to obsolete production technologies which are more labor-intensive. Instead, as a result of the closed cycle, lower wages lead to a drop in demand; in the following economic crisis (with the aid of unemployment) the relation between capital and labor restores itself. The necessity for more cost-efficiency and, consequently, for technological innovation doesn't change.

Therefore, it is neither the often-quoted foreign competition nor competition with the younger industrial nations which is the driving force in efforts to increase production, but the internal situation within all western industrial nations themselves (otherwise no one could explain what the causes for the dynamic in the competing countries are). The characteristic feature of our situation today is that many of the products which were previously responsible for growth and stimulated demand are reaching the saturation point of their market development. In other words, not enough basic innovations were undertaken early enough, although the need and the technology for them existed. Therefore the competitive situation of the industrial nations has changed.[4] They are no longer competing primarily in terms of selective and temporary advances in innovations with regard to products (product innovation), but in terms of differences in costs as a result of varying efforts made to improve cost efficiency (process innovation). A good example of this development is the Japanese car industry.

Overall, this development can be seen in the gap between the growth in production and productivity in the industrial nations (see Table 6-1), whereas in the past the growth rate of the GNP has been above the growth rate of worker productivity, thanks to increased demand caused by new products and consumption patterns.

For example, if economic policies remain unchanged in the Federal Republic of Germany, the growth in productivity will probably continue to outstrip that of production. The result is increasing unemployment, which at first sight will be caused by the use of new technologies, primarily microelectronics. This gap between the development of productivity and growth (which is not produced by new demand, but by labor-saving technical progress) is of particular importance since it represents a break in the cease-fire between the two sides of industry. In order to explain this, it is necessary to give a brief recapitulation of the historical background.

The world economic crisis in 1929 ended in Germany with the defeat of the labor movement and the victory of fascism. Following the military defeat of fascism, attempts were made in

TABLE 6-1
PRODUCTION OUTPUT AND PRODUCTIVITY ACCORDING TO SECTORS IN FOUR LARGE EUROPEAN COUNTRIES, 1963–73 AND 1973–77
(average annual growth rates in %)

Federal Republic of Germany

	Productivity growth 1963–73	Productivity growth 1973–77	Change in productivity growth	Change in production growth
1) Public administration	1.0	0	−1.0	−1.6
2) Agriculture	6.8	4.4	−2.4	−1.7
3) Industry	5.3	3.6	−1.7	−4.4
(Commerce)	(5.6)	(4.5)	(−1.1)	(−4.8)
4) Trade	3.7	0.2	−3.5	−5.8
5) Other activities	3.1	5.6	2.5	0.4
Total economy	4.6	3.2	−1.4	−3.1

Great Britain

	Productivity growth 1963–73	Productivity growth 1973–77	Change in productivity growth	Change in production growth
1) Public administration	−0.6	0.1	0.7	0.3
2) Agriculture	6.8	3.9	−2.9	−0.8
3) Industry	3.9	1.3	−2.6	−3.6
(Commerce)	(4.3)	(1.1)	(−3.2)	(−5.1)
4) Trade	3.5	−1.6	−5.1	−4.2
5) Other activities	2.5	0.5	−2.0	−2.3
Total economy	3.0	0.5	−2.5	−2.6

France

1) Public administration	1.9	2.3	0.4	−0.1
2) Agriculture	6.3	1.8	−4.5	−4.0
3) Industry	5.2	4.0	−1.2	−3.4
(Commerce)	(5.4)	(3.2)	(−2.2)	(−4.2)
4) Trade	2.7	1.3	−1.4	−3.0
5) Other activities	3.5	1.0	−2.5	−2.1
Total economy	4.6	2.7	−1.9	−2.7

Italy

1) Public administration	0.5	0.7	0.2	−0.6
2) Agriculture	6.9	4.3	−2.6	−0.4
3) Industry	5.6	0.8	−4.8	−4.1
(Commerce)*	(5.7)	(1.4)	(−4.3)	(−4.8)
4) Trade[†]	4.9	0.2	−4.7	−4.3
5) Other activities	3.5	3.3	−0.2	−1.7
Total economy	5.4	1.8	−3.6	−2.6

Agriculture includes agriculture, gamekeeping, forestry and fisheries.
Industry includes mining, quarrying, commerce, electricity, gas and water supply, and construction industry.
Trade includes wholesale and retail trade, catering and hotel industries.
* Including electricity, gas and water supply.
† Excluding catering and hotel industries.
Source: OECD Economic Outlook, July 1979

the Federal Republic of Germany to reconcile class antagonisms under the primacy of a market economy. Although the private control of capital remained untouched, it was considerably modified by two "social innovations": worker participation in management, and the obligation of the state to ensure full employment and growth (or rising mass incomes). It is largely thanks to this "historic compromise" that the Federal Republic of Germany today enjoys a relatively high level of prosperity, even on an international scale, and hence a politically important position in the relationship between Eastern and Western Europe.

This historic compromise in the social sphere is endangered today. Powerful forces are trying to undermine it under the cover of "supply-side economics," a conservative-liberal economic philosophy that postulates unemployment as inevitable—an argument that threatens to weaken decisively the position of the trade unions. Control of technological progress is to be left entirely in the hands of the employers; the workers themselves must bear the burden of adapting to changed conditions (change of job, loss of qualifications, inadequate working conditions). Fragmenting the labor market will remove the basis for a uniform representation of the workers' interests, leaving them manifestly powerless.

With this background in mind, it is clearly a matter of vital importance that the labor movement tackle two major tasks at once: first, it must maintain a high level of employment; second, it must work to ensure that both industry and society share the burdens caused by technological change. These two problem areas will be discussed below.

Effects of New Technologies on Employment Levels in Relation to Economic Policy Strategies

There is nothing in technological development—no "limits to growth"—that precludes a further growth of the world economy and full employment, at least in the industrial nations. Yet all these countries (Germany as well)[5] share signs of weakness:

- increasing shortage and rising price of raw materials and energy;
- increasing competition among the industrial nations and also between these and some developing countries with regard to capital goods;

- the fact that many products previously responsible for growth (cars, consumer goods with long service lives) are entering the market saturation phase;
- inflationary trends, currency fluctuations, instability of the international money markets;
- declining world market demand in the non-OPEC developing countries.

In many cases the key to solving these problems lies in applying new technologies. It must be said, however, that technological change demands structural change, usually within individual sectors of the economy. In other words, the technological change will lead to a devaluation of capital hitherto tied up in "outdated" technologies and to higher risks for investments made in new directions. In the final analysis, it is a political decision as to who bears the responsibility for the losses and risks.

The solution most often put foward is that the state should give up responsibility for full employment and concentrate all efforts on ensuring that the value of money remains stable. In Europe, Great Britain and Sweden provide examples of this policy. Such neoclassical strategies have also had an effect in the Federal Republic of Germany, although in diluted form, where responsibility for growth and employment lies mostly with the two sides of industry. The argument here is that wage restraint is necessary in order to improve company profits. This would lead to increased investments for expansion, but above all to cost-efficient improvement measures which would then lead to full employment.

This argument completely disregards the closed cycle. Wage restraint would first lead to a drop in demand which would take away the basis for expansion investments and high-risk innovations. The result would be a forced drive to improve cost-efficiency, which in turn would lead to a widening of the gap between productivity and demand, and therefore, would of necessity lead to unemployment as a result of technology. This development is very probable, especially since microelectronics presents a technological potential which would allow at least the large companies to cope with the *politically* generated pressure to improve cost-efficiency. Such a neoclassical program would mean that in coming years the Federal Republic of Germany can expect unemployment rates of approximately 10 percent.

A "Thatcher policy," moreover, would affect not only micro-electronics, but technological development in other fields as well. For example, the current pressure to innovate and invest would decrease for energy and raw materials technologies, because lower growth rates will cut the rate of consumption. Above all, technologies to conserve energy and raw materials would be developed and applied either hesitantly or not at all. One result: the oil shortage expected for the middle and late 1980s will create serious problems. In the absence of developed substitute technologies, governments will turn to atomic energy. The investment sums necessary will be enormous and would have to be made available very rapidly. In order not to increase inflation, this money can be raised only through wage cuts. Reduced wages, however, will rebound structurally on the consumer goods industry on the one hand, and on the energy consumption of the private households themselves on the other; in fact, for a while energy production and energy consumption may even go in opposite directions. At the same time, little use will be made of the opportunities for employment in decentralised energy technologies, insulating buildings, urban renewal, efficient use of raw materials and in new traffic systems.

Ironically, with a different economic policy these bottlenecks in the economic development of most industrial nations could be precisely those areas of supply and demand which make it possible to return to full employment. In the Federal Republic of Germany, for instance, a demand and investment potential would allow approximately 4 percent of the working population to be employed in these areas. The ultimate difference would be an 8 percent increase (about 1.5 million) in the working population—a measure of the different structural developments in the two policy concepts.

The basic economic policies of such growth and full employment can only be touched upon here. They are basically that the state should not simply create demand, but should make investments or provide incentives in key technological and economic sectors. These include energy and raw materials, housing and urban development, transport and traffic, the use of electronics and development of the working environment, and new social services.

Such a forward-looking structural policy contains elements of a strategy orientated to both supply and demand. In essence, the goal is to raise productivity above the present level by providing financial assistance for the use of microelectronics and, at the same time, to develop other areas of innovation and investment (which do not immediately increase productivity) in order to bring productivity and growth trends into line with one another. Unemployment as a result of technology, therefore, is not inevitable in the 1980s; technology itself supplies the incentives and instruments with which to achieve full employment.

Effects of Microelectronics on the Quality of the Work Place and Working Conditions

Sectors of the Economy and Vocational Groups Affected

It is obvious that technological change will be accompanied by disadvantages for many individual workers, although the extent of the disadvantage depends on developments in the labor market as a whole. The lower the unemployment, the more quickly and easily the worker or employee will find his way back into professional life. Technology, however, will affect certain sectors of the economy sooner and more seriously than others. Estimates indicate that in the Federal Republic of Germany microelectronics has been and will be the technology that brings about the greatest changes in work structures in offices and industry. Other technologies fall far behind in this regard.

Employment statistics indicate that during the next five years, there will be between 0.7 million and 2.5 million gainfully employed persons in those areas where rapid and considerable changes are most likely.[6] The proportion of persons within these areas whose jobs will actually be changed as a result of electronics cannot, however, be estimated. In this respect, the figures only represent an upper limit. But in the longer term, that is, in the next fifteen years, probably 50 percent of the total working population will find themselves in occupations changed, in one way or another, by electronics.

One characteristic effect of electronics on individual jobs will be the decline in importance of skills obtained during many years of experience, especially in the fields of light engineering and metal processing, but also in some crafts. This may be experienced in the form of a lowering of qualifications. In contrast, the ability to describe processes and transform them into program runs, as well as the ability to quickly comprehend new and unfamiliar relationships will gain in importance. In general, this is linked with more highly qualified activities (Tables 6-1 and 6-2 summarize the vocational groups that will be most affected in the next five years).

In addition to effects on individual professions and activities, microelectronics will also lead to structural changes in various sectors of the economy. Branches of industry directly affected by microelectronics include:

- the electrotechnical industry;
- data systems engineering;
- mechanical engineering;
- light engineering, optical engineering and horology;
- motor vehicle construction;
- aircraft construction;
- the steel processing industry;
- shipbuilding;
- the paper industry;
- the textile, clothing and footwear industries;
- the printing industry;
- the wood working and plastics processing industries;
- the chemicals industry.

It might have been easier to list sectors of the economy *not* affected; this list, however, serves to demonstrate the truly wide-ranging significance of microelectronics for industrial production. Furthermore, all office activities in general will be affected, as will tertiary economic sectors, including banking and insurance, trade, the press, legal and economic counselling, the mail, and science, education and art.

Trade Union Ideas on Overcoming the Technological Change

German trade unions have always stressed that they do not wish to pursue any policy having a generally inhibitive effect on technological change. In the past they have almost exclusively followed a policy of hardship compensation for work transfers and retraining for those affected by cost-efficiency improvements. This policy was accepted almost without exception by the members, for it involved no threat to full employment. Moreover, the trade unions had relatively extensive rights of participation in decision-making.

Both full employment and participation in decision-making were elements of the "historic compromise" among the labor movement, employers and the state. Conservative forces today question this historic compromise, but these essential trade union demands have not changed. Wage policy is also being reviewed with agreements to be negotiated on the following issues:

- working time (i.e. reduction of working life, working year and working week);
- protection in cases relating to cost-efficiency improvement measures;
- minimum work levels, minimum qualifications and production standards;
- safeguard qualifications (retraining into a job of equal value).

German trade unions continue to demand a greater role in personnel and job planning decisions, and they are increasingly concerned with participation in the shaping of research and technology policies.

Greater Humaneness in Working Life

In the past, many technological innovations led to a deterioration of working conditions. New technologies tended to use Tayloristic methods, which dehumanized work. Yet whatever the manner of its introduction, new technology always tends to change the organizational structure of a company and, consequently, the requirements imposed on the staff. In the past, workers and employees were usually the helpless victims of change; more recently, rising prosperity has changed attitudes toward working conditions.

Physical hardships (noise, dust, heat, the handling of toxic substances, heavy physical labor, and so on) have been recognized as characteristics of job quality for a long time; psychological strains (monotony of work, stress, etc.) are increasingly regarded in the same light. In fact, psychological strain often follows from the development of technologies and processes intended to re-

TABLE 6-2
VOCATIONAL GROUPS AFFECTED BY MICROELECTRONICS IN THE SHORT TERM

	Absolute 1976	Relative 1970 (1950 = 1)	Relative 1976 (1970 = 1)	Influencing subsidiary technology
1) Printers & setters	158,000	1.6	0.7	Integrated text processing, printing press control (above all, reduction of set-up times)
2) Welders, solderers, riveters	141,600	2.2	0.8	Automatic manipulators
3) Electricians, other mechanics	131,800	3.0	0.9	Assembly robots, greater degree of integration in structural components
4) Technical drawers, building drawers	107,600	3.3	0.9	Computer-assisted development and design
5) Laboratory assistants	94,600	2.0	0.9	Automatic analysis machines
6) Data processing experts	91,900	15.1	1.5	Software technology, very-large-scale integration
Total	726,200			

7)	Technicians	565,800	—	1.4	Computer assistance in development design, production planning and control
8)	Engineers	472,000	—	1.0	
9)	Secretaries, shorthand typists, audiotypists, data typists	417,100	2.0	0.9	Text processing and office communications systems
10)	Metal workers (cutting)	281,500	1.5	0.7	Program-controlled machine tools
11)	Metal workers (forming)	70,100	1.5	0.6	Automation of materials transport systems, manipulation systems
	Total	1,806,500			
	Overall total	2,532,700			

duce physical hardships. The industrial robot, for example, determines the rhythm and speed of human work output (man-machine relationship).

For most individuals, specialization resulting from the division of labor makes production processes less comprehensible; decision-making processes grow even more remote, and the general result is alienation from work. Individual creativity, motivation, readiness to take risks, and so forth, instead of being concentrated on work, focus on leisure activities.

Furthermore, inability to comprehend manifests itself in an increasing rejection of any type of large-scale technology. The expression "dinosaur technology" and the resistance of ever growing sections of the population to large industrial complexes and power stations (even outside the ranks of citizens' action groups) are all indicative of this attitude.

The starting points for developing and introducing comprehensible production processes can be both non-technological and technological. In many cases, the latter do not require any basically new solutions; rather, it is a case of using decentralized production technologies already available, for example in process heat, in small-scale steel works, and so forth. In many areas, microelectronics makes optimum production possible even in smaller businesses or small production series.

Non-technological solutions basically deal with problems of company organization and procedures such as management style, co-determination and degrees of freedom of individuals and groups in decision-making and business dealings. The importance of these aspects for research policy is taken into account in the program "Research into Making Working Life More Humane," which has been in force in the Federal Republic of Germany since 1974. Through this program the federal government provides assistance for research and development projects with the following aims:

- determining safety data, guidelines and minimum requirements for machines, plants and work places;
- developing work technologies adapted to human requirements;
- drawing up proposals and models to be used as examples for organizing work and designing work places;

• distributing and utilizating scientific findings and operational experiences.

Trade unions and employers' associations both participate in shaping this program, which is still in its infancy.

A number of possible solutions exist for reducing the psychological strains at work: group work to replace assembly-line work, job enrichment, job enlargement, job rotation, mechanization of monotonous work processes, use of robots, automatic manipulators, and more. Many of these approaches must be seen as first and not always successful attempts. Although psychological strains have decreased in many cases, other strains or combinations of strains have appeared—for instance, from working at display units, by taking over monitoring instead of production activities. These problems arise from inadequate knowledge of the "stress" phenomenon, of the factors that cause it and of the interactions between these factors. This is an important area for research.

There are also many possible solutions for avoiding or reducing physical hardships. To reduce noise, for example, motors may be encased, or thin noise-absorbent films with a molecular buffer-zone effect may be used. Similarly, there are also solutions for reducing other hardships (heat, dust, toxic substances and so forth).

A number of production processes are currently used to a limited extent, not only for reasons of cost, but also because of insufficient knowledge of their long-term effects on health. In addition to developing more dependable production processes with lower risks (instead of dealing with damage already caused), research is particularly needed in studying long-term effects and establishing appropriate scientific and empirical standards.

It is somewhat ironic that the main hope for humanizing industrial production lies in the appropriate use of industrial robots. Industrial robots are currently used in many fields: they manipulate tools (coating, spot-welding, continuous welding, deburring); they handle workpieces (in die-casting machines, injection moulding machines, die stamping, forging machines, etc.); they serve a variety of purposes in research and are of course valuable in assembly work. Types of robots range from simple equipment with a maximum of two working positions per axis all the way to equipment with six-axis continuous-path control.

The development of robot technology is intended to solve problems of positioning (by programming robots to imitate human movements), of drive (through high-efficiency disc armature motors), of grab systems (through self-adjusting flexible grab structures) and the problems of wear and long down times which still arise. Improvements in sensor systems (optoelectronic sensors), together with microprocessor technology (CAD technology) make it possible to use seeing, "intelligent" robots that can correct their own mistakes.

On the other hand, there are dangers in robot technology as well as resistance to it. The coming generation of intelligent robots threatens a mass displacement of labor in many areas. Moreover, the problem of the relationship between man and machine acquires a new dimension: man must work in step with the robot. Even though man is theoretically in command of the machine, the average worker will not feel in command—especially since industrial robots will further subdivide work processes, limiting the human worker to carrying out preliminary and finishing work for the robot.

There are also considerable risks in using microelectronics in both office technology and the services sector.

Information technology, in fact, has been described as a "technology for coordinating and controlling employees who defy Tayloristic organization." The need to replace typewriters with more text processing machines could mean that secretarial work could become even more strongly polarised: the majority of office employees would spend their entire time feeding typed material into machines, while a minority would occupy itself with more interesting administrative work. Some activities, on the other hand, will be upgraded. The demanding qualifications for software specialists provide an example, although the need for "systems analysis" could replace this form of expertise in a relatively short time.

Data processing is a newly created semiskilled profession that could lead to the elimination of conventional differences between workers and employees. The net effects on the welfare of the workers are less clear. The reduction of arduous work in physically hostile working environments is a plus, but must be weighed against the increased stress and pressure to be as productive as possible. The interaction between man and machine can lead to latter-day sweatshops. "Intelligent terminals," for example, extend the potential for supervising and controlling workers. Electronic cash registers, for example, can be constructed to register automatically the working speed of the operating personnel, the number of mistakes and the effective working time. The ergonomic problems connected with technology have now become the subject of various trade-union investigations. One particular problem is the increasing eye fatigue related to the use of visual display units.

The program "to make working life more humane" is intended to prevent office work from becoming more Tayloristic. Its aims include avoiding physical and psychological strains (caused by visual display units, for example) by means of suitable technical and organizational developments, improving the quality and variety of work places, and increasing the degree of creative freedom by the development of appropriate equipment and systems.

Unfortunately, many companies and administrative bodies today still see the aim and the program as a social pastime. They also argue that it adversely affects international competitiveness and economic productivity. These arguments are not new. They have been used against all concrete improvements of working conditions, against the abolition of child labor, the introduction of accident prevention legislation, the introduction of the eighthour day and the introduction of co-determination on management boards. In the end, reforms have always proved beneficial: labor productivity has increased, not decreased.

In coming years microelectronics will make cheap "artificial intelligence" available in many areas, resulting in greater and different demands on the worker in virtually all aspects of the economy and administration. The worker not only must bring knowledge and ability to his work, but also the specifically human qualities of independence, responsibility, and creativity. Such characteristics, however, cannot be developed under autocratic conditions in which one side gives orders and the other obeys.

Notes

1. David S. Landes, *The Unbound Prometheus* (London: Cambridge University Press, 1969), p. 442.

2. Landes, chs. 6 and 7.

3. Prognos AG/Mackintosh Consultants Company Ltd., *Technischer Fortschritt, Auswirkungen auf Wirtschaft und Arbeitsmarkt* [Important Technological Developments and Their Significance for Economic Application], vol. 1 (Basel & Luton, 1979).

4. OECD, *Science and Technology in the New Socio-Economic Context* (Paris: OECD Publications, 1979), pp. 125–136.

5. Prognos AG/Mackintosh, pp. 47–69; Diethard B. Simmert, ed., *Wirtschaftspolitik-kontrovers* (Bonn, 1979).

6. Bundesministerium für Forschung und Technologie [Federal Ministry for Research and Technology], *Gesprächskreis Modernisierung der Volkswrirtschaft, Elektronik, Produktivität, Arbeitsmarkt* (Bonn, 1979); Prognos AG/Mackintosh; Europaisches Gewerkschaftsinstitut [European Institute for Trade Unions], *Die Auswirkungen der Mikroelektronik auf die Beschäftigung in West-europa während der achtziger Jahre* (Brussels, 1979).

7

Plant Closings and Economic Dislocations

European Experience and American Prospects

BRIAN TURNER

Brian Turner is executive assistant to the president of the Industrial Union Department, AFL-CIO, and the IUD's director of legislation and economic policy.

He addresses the changes in American industrial structure, increasingly characterized by oligopolies, concentration of ownership, and multinational ownership. The result has been an epidemic of plant closings in the United States during the 1970s. Turner contrasts the Western European response to similar problems with the United States' lack of any effective, comprehensive policy or program to salvage the individuals, communities, and regions left jobless. He points out that Germany, Japan and Sweden have managed to combine high growth rates with high degrees of economic security and makes a plea for American reindustrialization policies based on equity and efficiency. He concludes that under the present administration such prospects are grim.

PLANT CLOSINGS AND ECONOMIC DISLOCATIONS: European Experience and American Prospects

Brian Turner

Over the past decade the United States has experienced an acceleration in plant closings accompanied by America's customary unwillingness to address the problem adequately. It doesn't have to be that way. Last year's report by the Steelworkers, Auto Workers, and Machinists team, *Economic Dislocation*,[1] provides ready proof that the advanced, industrial societies of Europe can treat workers as human beings in the face of economic change. The domestic counterpart of their work is the comprehensive study, *Capital and Communities*, by Barry Bluestone and Bennett Harrison.[2] Their book provides a riveting account of the social tragedy of plant closings and a compelling brief for the defense of millions of workers threatened by unaccountable, unilateral decisions from the corporate boardroom.

On November 5, 1980, however, the nation awoke to the reality of Ronald Reagan's election. The standard-bearer for the extreme right wing of America's business-oriented party will seek to move the United States still further away from humane and efficient processes for dealing with plant closings—and from humane solutions to other social and economic problems as well. With only 50.7 percent of the national vote these ideologists of

119

"free market forces" claim a mandate for a return to the economic prescriptions of 200 years ago.

To develop and then implement a policy for plant closings, as in many other areas of urgent need, we will have to return to basics for a rebuilding period: we must educate, organize the unorganized, and—sometimes the most challenging—organize the organized for political action. It is helpful to examine both what has worked in other countries and what foundation the American experience provides for action here. This paper starts with a review of European programs for plant closings, turns to a survey of the limited existing protections against plant closings in this country, and finally analyzes lines of action for building a more secure, more equitable future for working Americans.

European Experience

Although Americans cannot "import" policies and institutions from Europe, we can learn from other advanced capitalist countries that, by and large, have coped more successfully with a wide range of economic and social problems. Much of what has worked well in Europe could be wisely adapted for application in the United States. What we need to understand most is that the European approaches combine good human and economic sense.

Framework of Social Institutions and Policy

In Europe, support for economic and employment policies is derived from an institutional framework in which the interests of ordinary working people are far more strongly represented than in the United States. The European countries with the most successful economic track records are those whose unions represent 45, 65, or 85 percent of the labor force—compared to some twenty-five percent in this country. Complementing these generally robust labor movements are relatively strong democratic socialist parties, either in power or strongly influencing national policy during the past several decades. These institutional differences, with their own deep historical roots, help explain sharp differences in economic and employment policies.

The background for dislocation policies in Europe is provided by a framework of effective general economic management coupled with active employment and social policies. Throughout the sixties and early seventies most European economies were managed at or near full employment, with unemployment rates of 2, 3, or 4 percent, compared with 5, 6, 7, 8 or 9 percent in this country. European recessions tend to be less frequent and less severe.

The framework of social legislation—health care, child care, social security, and so forth—has in general been superior to that provided in the United States. The United States, for example, is the only advanced industrial country (excluding South Africa) which does not have national health insurance.

European employment policies—unemployment compensation, assistance programs and labor market policies to promote reemployment—provide high-level assistance in cushioning unemployment and promoting adjustment to new jobs. Unemployment compensation normally runs from seventy to eighty percent of total compensation in prior employment; in cases of mass dislocation or in targeted industries, income support can run up to ninety percent of pre-separation wages for several years or even longer. Active employment service programs assist workers in locating new employment opportunities, travelling for job interviews and defraying the costs of moving to a new job. Training plays a key role in the logic of European unemployment/adjustment programs. In Sweden, which possesses "active labor market policies," up to three percent of the national work force may be in training at any one time; this helps explain how a two percent unemployment rate can be maintained over many years. In Germany unemployed workers have a right to three years of training when they are unemployed. The goal is to reverse the typical effects of protracted unemployment. With good training for needed skills, workers can re-enter the work force with greater skill, higher productivity and improved earning power.

Relatively advanced industrial and regional policies guide the European national economies toward higher productivity, higher skill, and higher wage industries. Industrial policy promotes expansion of industries with the strongest futures, without having to rely on wasteful general business tax cuts when the objective is to stimulate a handful of targeted industries. On the other hand, special programs operate to facilitate worker and community adjustment in industries losing employment, such as shipbuilding or apparel.

The evolution of this system is monitored through various forms of co-determination at the company and plant level. Workers and their unions meet regularly with management and have full access to company information relevant to employment-related decision-making. These company and plant level processes tend to complement the national procedures for tripartite consultation or consensus-building on economic and social policy, where labor, business, and government seek to work out solutions that make sense to all concerned.

Plant Closings Provisions

European systems for dealing with plant closings vary somewhat from country to country, but each national system represents a variation on a common set of themes. Rather than deal with the moderate variations from country to country, we can best deal with a hypothetical but useful "general European economic dislocation policy" which represents the main outlines of European approaches as seen from the United States.

Advance notice

Early warning of major layoffs is a prerequisite for any meaningful dislocation policy. The suddenness and the extent of job loss is what makes a plant closing so difficult for workers and communities to cope with. Advance notice provides the breathing space required for either finding alternatives to the plant closing or controlling the timing of the job loss so that the impact on the community will be minimized and reemployment prospects maximized. In every European system thirty to ninety days is the minimum advance notice required for economic dislocations of any sort; larger layoffs generally require longer periods of advance notice. In some countries one year's advance notice is becoming the norm. Typically, notice must be given to the government and its employment service agencies, to the union and workers council, and to individual workers who may be affected.

Consultation and Negotiation

One of the first steps taken after an advance notice is for the workers and their union to sit down with management. Both sides examine ways to avoid layoffs while dealing with the economic difficulty presumably faced by the firm. They might discuss new lines of business, staggered working hours, handling layoffs through attrition, or other measures. At the same time the government employment service will be reviewing the proposed layoff with management to ascertain whether it is indeed necessary. Government representatives may have suggestions of their own to solve the problem.

Social plan

If layoffs cannot be avoided through these consultations, the firm and its union representatives develop a plan to ease the social transition—for the directly affected workers, for the community and for the many workers in local service industries indirectly affected by mass layoffs. Under a negotiated "social plan," layoffs may be staged over a period of months to minimize the impact on the labor market; workers may be put on short time with the government unemployment insurance system picking up seventy-five percent of the wages for the lost hours (as in Germany); and priorities can be established for the workers affected, which typically protect older workers, workers with family responsibilities, and workers facing special difficulties in relocating.

Focused government action

Government uses the period of advanced notice to focus its relevant services on the threatened locality or plant. Extra employment service personnel may be brought in; Sweden, for example, sometimes installs a computer terminal in the affected facility listing job openings around the country. Public works projects may be started to provide temporary local employment; the government may attempt to attract new business to the area (typically using capital investment subsidies in the affected locality) or undertake special training efforts for the work force. Meanwhile, the standard employment service attempts to match workers and their skills with new employment opportunities.

A second level of government support may be mobilized for job losses in industries suffering long-term decline or very large-scale dislocations. In these cases the level of income support will rise to eighty or ninety per cent of the pre-separation wage. Early retirement at full pension is available for older workers. In addition, workers may receive substantial lump sum severance payment, known as the "golden handshake," amounting to some tens of thousands of dollars for workers with long tenure in industries undergoing major contractions.

The American Landscape—Current Experience

If Americans perceive this sketch of European practices as they might a vision through the looking glass, they will find it educational to listen to European manufacturers who have been investing more and more in American production facilities: "Why have European multinationals been flocking to this country? In America, when demand for our products goes down, we simply lay workers off. In Europe business doesn't have that kind of freedom." America is the only major industrial country to violate the most important canon of the ILO constitution: it treats its workers as commodities to be employed or discarded depending on business conditions.

Of all the industrialized Western nations, the United States allows business the most freedom to lay workers off in the face of weak demand. It is the least interventionist, generally leaving workers and communities to what conservative economists boast of as "the free play of market forces." It is the least active in targeting industrial policies to complement macroeconomic management, either for promoting future high growth industries or for easing and guiding industrial, community, regional, and individual adjustments in the face of economic change. Finally, it possesses the least developed dislocation policy. A small group of very incomplete government programs deals with only limited categories of dislocations, and even then only with limited parts of the problem. The result is predictable: Americans suffer probably the highest levels of damage from plant closings and economic dislocations while its general economic support systems are by far the weakest among the industrial countries.

Scope and Dynamics of Plant Closings and Dislocation in the United States

The extreme vulnerability of American society and its workers is more than a product of the size of its economy and the lack of coherent dislocation policies. It stems from the basic structure of American industry and the logical evolution of that structure over time.

Industrial Structure

Since World War II the industrial structure of the American economy has evolved in three parallel directions, all of which result in increases both in corporate power and the likelihood of plant closings and relocations: first, increasing size and concentration; second, advancing multinationalization; and third, growing conglomerate organization. At the time of the formation of America's great industrial unions during the late 1930s, American industry was dominated by large nationally integrated companies operating essentially in a single industry. U.S. Steel, General Motors, General Electric and Standard Oil are typical examples. Today comparable companies are far larger and far more dominant in their primary industries; monopoly and oligopoly are becoming the rule in more industries every year. Economic concentration has advanced to the point where the 500 largest corporations now control 70 percent of total manufacturing employment. In a further qualitative transformation, we see these corporate giants now operating in many countries as multinationals, thereby exploiting American tax laws and past technological advantages. And we see these conglomerate multinational companies operating in many industries, pushed on by the attractions of financial diversification and the financial and tax rewards of cross-subsidization from one line of business to another, from one country to another. All these basic changes in industrial structure enormously increase a company's ability and proclivity to shift production locations.

In addition, revolutions in the communications and transportation industries have vastly increased corporate mobility. The links between production sites and consumption markets have been broken forever. On a global scale this has produced an internationalization of industry and competition, including the growth of multinationals based in Europe, Japan, Brazil, and elsewhere with further implications for increased plant closings and relocations.

Each of these structural changes, of course, has increased industrial mobility while undermining the power of labor relative to capital. It is not accidental that American unions have declined from roughly 35 percent of the labor force in 1953 to some 25 percent today. During the seventies business has found it more attractive to move to sunnier climates with weaker unions. More recently they have begun an overt assault on labor, our national labor law, and the consuming and tax-paying public.

These basic structural changes have accelerated in the past decade. The energy price surge since the 1973–74 oil embargo has increased the pressure for changes in industrial stucture and location for all energy users, which is to say virtually all sectors of today's economy. And skyrocketing energy prices, starting from an artificially low base, have spurred inflation mistakenly and vainly countered by general anti-inflation policies. Fiscal and monetary restriction have not reduced inflation, but they have indeed produced recession, record unemployment, and high interest rates which made the prices of all interest-dependent products—notably housing—skyrocket still further. The result has been not only stagnation, but plant closings and failures at an epidemic rate.

Extent of the problem

Plant closings cut across every industry and every region of the country. The steel industry lost nearly 30,000 jobs in one month of 1978 because of plant closings, and in 1980 lost still more; old industrial towns like Youngstown, Ohio and Lackawanna, New York were hit hard, but so were newer sites like Fontana, California. In the last five years, the electronics industry has lost major facilities in every area of production; major closings in color television production alone have hit small towns like Batavia and Horseheads, New York and Albion, Michigan as well as major urban areas like Chicago, Illinois and Jersey City, New

Jersey. In the last two to three years the rubber industry has lost nearly 40,000 jobs, mainly through plant closings, in Detroit, Michigan and Akron, Ohio and other tire plants throughout the country. The disappearance of a good part of the auto industry and its jobs from the pressure of high gasoline prices and Japanese imports has destroyed some of the most modern plants in the industry, like the nearly brand-new Fairmont assembly plant in Mahwah, New Jersey. Over 100 plant closings have been reported by auto parts unions other than the UAW, with most of these job losses occurring in small towns throughout the midwest, the east coast, the south and the west. Metal fabrication shops, forges and stamping plants, and non-ferrous metal smelting and fabrication have been deeply hurt by plant closings during the 1970s, losing plants in Oregon, Idaho, Arizona, New Mexico, Connecticut, Rhode Island, throughout the states in the Ohio valley and in virtually every other part of the country as well. Textile plants and apparel shops have lost tens of thousands of jobs through closings in the last few years alone. The losses continue across the spectrum of American industry.

Of course the phenomenon of plant closing extends far beyond manufacturing industries. In retail and wholesale trade, for instance, dozens of A & P supermarkets have been closed in recent years. And within the last eighteen months the Korvettes chain and its sixty-odd stores have disappeared from the map; some of these stores may reappear in the near future, under different management and without a union contract. Transportation has also been hard hit. The Railway Express company and its 25,000 workers have gone the way of the Pony Express. Railroads, bus lines and airlines have suffered substantial job loss through takeovers, mergers, and outright failures.

How many plant closings are occurring throughout the United States in total? Barry Bluestone and Bennett Harrison estimate an average rate of some 2.5 million jobs per year destroyed by closings.[3] (The authors use 1969–76 data.) That means, projected across the decade of the 1970s, 25,000,000 jobs destroyed through shutdown alone. To illustrate the enormous scale of this phenomenon, that 25,000,000 equals more than one-fourth the total number of workers in the United States labor force. And this trend shows no sign of weakening.

Partial Systems—Special Assistance in the United States

The United States has *no* policies and programs dealing with plant closings as such. In fact there exists only a handful of *ad hoc* special adjustment programs for workers who lose their jobs as a result of specific public policy actions; these include decisions that dramatically increase imports (Trade Adjustment Assistance), the conversion of a single logging area to a Redwood National Park, the consolidation of separate railroads (the so-called AMTRAK formula) and airlines, and reorganization of federally supported mass transit systems. The one small United States program geared toward closings *per se* applies only to elimination of military bases (and in some cases to closings of military production facilities).

The contrast with European approaches could hardly be greater. The common thread running through the American programs is the protection—very weak protection—of limited groups of workers from the economic harm expected to result from specific public policy actions. These are actually not "dislocation" or "plant-closing" policies, but rather part of the price for achieving unrelated policy goals. The serious problems caused by plant closings are not even addressed in these special-purpose programs.

Another measure of these special-purpose programs is the size of the population they serve. Trade Adjustment Assistance (TAA) has served some 400,000 workers in six years of operation (that is, since its revision in 1974; only 30,000 received benefits under the earlier TAA system that ran from 1962 to 1974), for an average of less than 70,000 per year. The Redwood Park legislation targeted only 600 workers. And the rail and airline consolidation protections, urban mass transit, and other special-purpose programs together have served less than 100,000 workers in the past fifteen years. Compare these figures with the 2,500,000 jobs lost to plant closings yearly, or the 20,000,000 who leave their jobs through plant closings or other causes in a given year. The numbers speak for themselves.

Why is special effort to alleviate dislocation and promote readjustment in plant closings warranted? Because the loss of hundreds or thousands of jobs at one time in one location is not the same as individual job losses scaled up by several orders of magnitude. The social impact of mass joblessness—increased crime, suicide, homicide, psychiatric problems, domestic violence, and alcohol and drug dependence—can be staggering. In Union City, Indiana, for example, three auto-parts plants closed during 1979–80, raising unemployment to 30 percent; this same year has seen a 56 percent increase in defaulted credit, a 120 percent rise in bankruptcies and evictions, a 69 percent rise in burglary and theft, and a 530 percent increase in outlays for food stamps. One study reports a tripled suicide rate among workers who lost their jobs due to plant closings.[4]

The most immediate impact of plant closings is the difficulty workers have in finding a decent new job in a labor market flooded with hundreds of job-seekers with similar backgrounds and skills. When two New England shoe factories closed, for instance, 40 percent of the workers were still unemployed two years later. The difficulty of finding new jobs contrasts paradoxically with the main feature of American special-purpose programs: They contain little or no provisions to facilitate adjustment to new jobs. Their main emphasis is on income maintenance—surely a vital concern for the affected worker and his or her family—but temporary income maintenance with no provision for new work is poor recompense for the victims of plant closings.

Income maintenance is necessary for dislocation adjustment systems because of the general weakness of United States unemployment compensation. In contrast with European practice, UC payments in this country range from 30 to 59 percent of pre-separation wages and last from 15 to 30 weeks, depending on state practices. (Extended unemployment compensation benefits for an additional 13 weeks can be triggered by high national and state unemployment rates). These levels are too low and the durations too short for general unemployment problems, much less those resulting from plant closings. In recessionary years literally millions of American workers exhaust their UC payments without finding new work.

Income maintenance under Trade Adjustment Assistance, by far the largest special-purpose program, is raised to 70 percent of prior wages and extended to one full year (an additional twenty-six weeks is available to workers over sixty and to workers in training). Under the smaller special-purpose programs income may be fully maintained for periods up to six years.

The special-purpose adjustment programs in the United States simply fail to bring new jobs to impacted areas or to train workers for new skills. There are statutory provisions for training, but the funds aren't there. In the first two years of the TAA program, for instance, less than one-half of 1 percent of TAA recipients were enrolled for training. Whether their unemployment is short term or long term, the programs have not made the commitment to restoring relevant skills and meaningful earning power to those whose lifelong investment in work skills has been destroyed by a plant closing.

Attracting new industry to areas hit by plant closings is the job of the Commerce Department's Economic Development Administration (EDA), but their targeting is diffused through a majority of the countries in the various states. Their assistance to localities is largely concentrated in public works and infrastructure investments—industrial parks, rail and highway links, and so on. More active approaches of attracting private investment are limited and underutilized. (Ironically, the Economic Development Administration is scheduled for extinction in the Reagan "free enterprise" program.)

The absence of a readjustment focus in these special purpose programs—and indeed in all American policy in this area—is exemplified by the absence of any advance notice provision in United States law. As a result, even the special-purpose programs typically arrive on the scene with income support and modest adjustment provisions many months after job losses or plant closings have occurred. In the Trade Adjustment Assistance program, for instance, there is a ten-month backlog in the processing of petitions which may be filed only *after* jobs have been lost. Assistance that arrives ten months or more after workers have been laid off can hardly be called assistance for adjustment. In fact, it is commonly called "burial insurance," because the patient is long since dead by the time the help arrives.

Negotiated provisions in union contracts are relatively new and generally provide rudimentary protections. While 75 percent of all union contracts do call for advance notice of plant closings, 81 percent of these call for advance notice of one week or less. For income protection beyond the meager provisions of unemployment compensation and the often late coverage of Trade Adjustment Assistance, only 16 percent of union contracts provide for supplementary unemployment benefits (SUB), and only ten percent of the workers covered by large contracts are eligible for SUB.

The absence of national health insurance in the United States compounds the losses from protracted unemployment resulting from plant closings. Few union contracts provide for extentions of health insurance coverage, and those that do provide extended coverage for only a few months. Likewise, lost pension and social security contributions are not compensated in the United States, in contrast with Europe. Of course, under all this lies the woefully inadequate system of unemployment compensation.

The absence of democratic planning to deal with threatened mass layoffs and to minimize the social damage resulting from plant closings is perhaps the most telling aspect of America's present non-response to the problem of plant closings. In only a very few cases, for instance in the new Steelworker contract negotiated in 1980, can we find mechanisms for involving workers and their unions in planning these painful adjustment decisions. There are a few extraordinary cases where companies have voluntarily participated in such planning. These few cases—including the closing by the Studebaker Automobile Company, the Armour Meat Packing Company, and recently Brown and Williamson Tobacco—indicate that American companies do have the capability in concert with their unions to soften the blows of these economic disasters for their workers and their communities. Why, then cannot all companies act in such a human and democratic manner? And if they can, why shouldn't they be required to do so by law?

Current Prospects

The immediate prospects for changing this dismal picture on plant closings and dislocation are dim. Excellent legislation has been introduced, but with the change in control of the White House and the Senate, and with a further shift to the right in the

House of Representatives, labor and its allies must move into a period of long-term rebuilding, including sharper definition on economic and social policy positions.

Such a period of rebuilding will cover not only economic and social policy formulations, but all aspects of organization, communication, outreach, and more extensive coalition building. This challenge of organizational and policy rebuilding is all the more urgent given the certainty that Republican ideological and macroeconomic efforts to revive the economy will not only be inequitable, but almost certainly will fail. The decontrol of oil and gas while "unshackling" capitalism through business tax cuts and destroying regulatory protections will only increase inflation without putting the nine or ten million jobless Americans back to work. The advocates for workers, the retired, the poor, the minorities, the disenfranchised must be in a position to challenge these Republican wolves in their poorly disguised sheeps' clothing. We must be prepared to act on the common ground among us: our desire to rebuild our economy, put America back to work, and achieve a more fair, just, and democratic society.

We cannot wait passively for Reagan to fail. It will not be long before Americans realize that Republican economic policies from Ronald Reagan will be at least as inadequate as the functionally Republican economic policies of the preceding administration. And we must be ready with a comprehensive, sensible and effective program.

The pending plant closings bills provide part of this overall approach. They fill the gaps so painfully obvious in our brief review of present practice. The Ford-Riegle Bill (first introduced in substance in 1975 by then Senator Mondale and Congressman Ford) is the best vehicle. It calls for

- advance notice from six months to two years for all major layoffs and closings;
- improved income maintenance for affected workers;
- protection of fringe benefits;
- substantial training and related services for laid-off workers;
- assistance for transferring facilities to new owners, particularly to workers and community members;
- loan guarantees and technical assistance to prevent plant closings where feasible;

• tax liabilities on the firm to be given local governments to compensate for substantial adjustment costs imposed on the community.

Additional provisions should (but at present do not) include establishing democratic planning committees to find ways of avoiding layoffs where feasible and to make necessary adjustments as smooth as possible.

The challenge in constructing compelling reindustrialization policies, including such adjustment policies, lies in justifying them not only on grounds of equity, but on grounds of their efficiency in strengthening our economy. The traditional emphasis of labor and related groups has been on the side of equity. But in today's climate, faced with pressing economic problems, arguments of equity must be joined by strong arguments of efficiency. The reindustrialization proposals recently articulated by the AFL-CIO do this by establishing democratic tripartite procedures (panels of representatives from labor, business and government) for allocating needed investment capital including pension fund capital where market mechanisms and macroeconomic instruments have clearly failed. Equity and efficiency must go hand-in-hand.

The same overlapping of equity and efficiency should prevail in dislocation and plant closing policies. Advance notice allows labor (and capital) to minimize idleness and thus to increase output, productivity and efficiency. Job creation strategies avoid cutbacks and failures in local service and supply industries by bringing new jobs to the laid-off workers rather than by moving workers to jobs elsewhere. Serious job search and relocation assistance can improve the efficiency of labor markets while reducing the pain and the duration of unemployment. Substantial training opportunities for the long-term unemployed—whether from plant closings or other causes—can improve the capability of our work force to do the jobs of the 1980s and 1990s, jobs requiring higher skills and more specialized training.

These sensible policies are all the more important now that the American politicians and economists in power are calling for the imagined glories of eighteenth- or nineteenth-century capitalism; they have failed to learn from contemporary European experience. Europe, with higher levels of business taxation, has higher productivity growth and lower inflation. Does it follow that the United States needs to further lower taxes to solve its economic problems?

The most important variable ignored by the "supply side" politicians is how labor affects productivity and economic competitiveness. The three industrialized countries with the highest rates of productivity growth, to take perhaps the most relevant indicator, are the three countries with the highest levels of economic security for workers. In Japan, with the highest rates of productivity growth, full-time employees enjoy lifetime employment security, and therefore almost unshakeable economic security. Sweden and Germany, the two industrial countries next highest in productivity growth, provide economic security through barriers to layoffs, through active labor market policies, and through general economic management which genuinely seeks to maintain full employment and minimize the threat of unemployment.

In addition, Germany and Sweden (and through different mechanisms, Japan) involve their workers as human beings in the running of their industrial enterprises. Their workers are not treated like machines during production, nor are they casually discarded when demand for production falls off. The notion that economic security in these countries helps strengthen their productivity and competitiveness is confirmed by American experiments in improving the quality of work life and productivity. All the successful American productivity experiments are predicated on the economic security of the participating workers, and on strong democratic participation by workers and their unions in plant and assembly-line economic decision-making.

Economic security from the threat of plant closings and mass layoffs is one vital step on the road toward a revitalized and more human economy for the United States. This country faces a choice, one it must make soon: between exposing workers more and more to nineteenth-century pressures and insecurities, or providing them with more security, dignity, and participation in democratic control over their own lives at work. The evidence from Europe and elsewhere in the contemporary industrial world indicates that there is only one successful solution.

Notes

1. *Economic Dislocation—Plant Closings, Plant Relocation, and Plant Conversions* (United Auto Workers, United Steel Workers of America, International Association of Machinists, 1979).
2. Barry Bluestone and Bennett Harrison, *Capital and Communities* Washington, D.C.: Progressive Alliance, 1980).
3. Ibid., p. 59.
4. D. d'Ambrosio, Allied Industrial Workers of America, Testimony before United States International Trade Commission, 1980.

PART III

Workers' Participation

8

Worker Participation in Europe

CLIVE JENKINS

Clive Jenkins is general secretary of the Association of Scientific, Technical, and Managerial Staffs (ASTMS) and a member of the British Trades Union Congress (TUC) General Council. He was a member of the Committee of Enquiry into Industrial Democracy (known as the Bullock Committee), which was set up by the Labour government in 1975.

In this paper Jenkins presents the basic philosophy and drive behind the demands for increased workers' participation in the management of their workplaces. He then outlines the range of recent Western European approaches—works councils, worker directors, extension of collective bargaining, development of planning agreements. He concludes that though methods vary for increasing workers' access to economic decision-making in Western Europe, the intent is the same: democratization of industry and of the economy in general.

WORKER PARTICIPATION IN EUROPE

Clive Jenkins

"The coming of age of democracy in our society is a process that inevitably affects the whole of people's lives; it cannot be excluded from the workplace."—Committee of Enquiry into Industrial Democracy, U.K., 1975.

There is a natural and growing demand, all over the world, for greater public participation in decision-making processes at all levels of government and in all aspects of society. The periodic right to cast one's vote in free democratic elections no longer offsets the daily experience of autocracy in the working environment—if it ever did.

People spend a major part of their time at work—their livelihoods depend on it—and this time strongly influences their quality of life. That they should seek to participate in the decision-making processes both on the shop floor and on the plant, company and board level is neither surprising nor subversive.

Participation by workers in the decisions that affect their employment necessarily extends to the strategic decisions taken at board level. It is here, if not at a lower level, that workers' aspirations sometimes conflict with those of government. This is especially the case in the relatively small number of large multiplant enterprises which dominate the economy, whether in public or private ownership. The extension of worker participation in this context amounts to a movement toward a potentially tripartite (management, government and trade-union) decision-making process.

In the United Kingdom there is a long standing and widely perceived failure on the part of industry to deliver the goods in terms of wages and job security for the workforce. Production output, exports and living standards have all suffered. A long period of inadequate capital formation has left a poorly adapted industrial structure; new technology is usually introduced as part of a strategy for industrial contraction. It is hardly surprising that the current recession has proved devastating.

These failures have strengthened the desire of workers for a greater measure of participation, and their desire is matched by that of Labour politicians for a greater measure of economic planning and control. Current discussion between the TUC and the Labour party recognizes that progress in both of these areas could be mutually supportive. The new planning framework envisaged provides for systematic inputs from workers and their trade union representatives.

While workers' participation is normally argued as an infringement upon the "right to manage," the underlying question, of course, is the "rights of ownership." Pension funds have been increasingly portrayed as an adequate form of "workers' ownership"—but this is a thin and irrelevant argument against democratizing management and increasing both worker and government participation.

The Case for Worker Participation

The last twenty years have seen the growth of the giant industrial enterprise and the concentration of economic power in the hands of fewer and fewer companies. In the United Kingdom, for example, whereas in 1953 the 100 largest manufacturing enterprises accounted for 25 percent of total net output, by 1971 the corresponding figure was 40 percent. The work force of these firms is counted in tens of thousands. As companies have grown in size and complexity they have also tended to become remote from the communities in which they operate and from the people whom they employ. Major decisions about the nature of a company's or a plant's organization—decisions that closely affect the local community as well as the employees—are commonly made far away from the site by the directors of a parent or holding company, and often by the management of a parent company overseas.

The power and complexity of the industrial enterprise and the remoteness of decision-making have led to demands that large companies become more responsive to the needs of society in general and of their employees in particular. Industry is coming under pressure to consider the wider effects of the decisions it takes in pursuit of profit, and it is beginning to respond. To a great extent this is a recognition of the increasing influence of employees and their trade unions, but it is also an acceptance of the principle that a socially responsible company in a democratic society cannot operate without taking account of the interests and the opinions of its employees.

On their part, employees who invest their labor in a company are no longer content to have their future decided by people over whom they have no control. They want a say in how their workplace is run and in all the decisions affecting its future, including areas such as investment planning, price policy and so forth, which have hitherto been regarded as matters of management prerogative. These desires are reinforced by trade union organization of white-collar workers, including engineers and managers. Paternalism and autocracy have had their day; employees now feel that their working life must be democratized. Workers' participation—or industrial democracy—is a means of ensuring that workers' interests are taken into account in the decision-making process.

Recent years, then, have witnessed the emergence of worker participation as a major issue for debate. Legislation on worker directors (and broadly comparable schemes) has been introduced or amended in at least seven European countries since 1970, and serious discussion of such possibilities has occurred in several others. An important factor influencing the debate has been the EEC commission's proposed Fifth Directive on company law. Published in 1972, it proposes employee representation on company supervisory boards. The commission is now revising the directive to take into account the enlargement of the community, but also widespread employer resistance. There are other factors adding impetus to discussions about worker participation, including a better educated and more powerful work force (often due to greatly enlarged union organization), and rapid rates of industrial and technical change. Equally important is the economic crisis in many European countries, which is characterized by high rates of inflation that outstrip the rise in real wages, high levels of unemployment and major structural problems resulting from the widespread introduction of low-cost high technology in information technology.

The Meaning of Industrial Democracy

The term "industrial democracy" implies a form of suffrage similar to that in political life, with workers being able to change the "government" in industry and to participate directly in management decisions. In practice, industrial democracy usually means a more limited form of influence and involvement, including the receipt of information or joint consultation as well as the inclusion of workers on the board. It is also used by some to describe workers' shareholding schemes (which do not give workers any real share in the power of the firm and which could put their savings and pensions at risk, as well as their jobs, if the firm collapses, as happened with Rolls Royce in 1970) and methods of improving the quality of working life. These include direct participation in decisions involving job rotation, job enlargement, job enrichment, autonomous work groups, work restructuring, and so forth. Their potential for increasing worker participation in industry-wide decision-making, however, is extremely limited.

The varying definitions of the term "industrial democracy" reflect varying philosophies and priorities. The most radical views insist that major structural changes in society are an essential precondition of any meaningful industrial democracy; therefore it is pointless to participate in management under the current social order. Such a view underlies the practice of self-management in Yugoslavia and a number of trade unions in Europe; the CGT (General Labor Confederation) in France for one example. This view surfaced in France in 1968 during the widespread student unrest and workers' occupation of factories.

When General de Gaulle promised greater participation in industry and society for instance, this poster appeared on Paris walls:

> I participate
> You participate
> He participates
> We participate
> You participate
> They profit!

Other, less radical views accept the capitalist structure of society but reject involvement in management in the belief that trade unions can best defend and promote workers' interests by collective bargaining and by acting as a permanent and independent opposition.

Trade Unions in Europe

Worker participation in European countries largely reflects the different histories and traditions of the respective trade unions and their relations with industry in these countries. The British labor movement is the oldest in the world, the product of the first industrial revolution in history. A mixture of independent craft, occupational, white-collar, sectoral, industrial and general unions has evolved under the umbrella organization of the TUC (Trades Union Congress). The TUC, however, possesses only such powers as are delegated to it by the constituent unions, which maintain their own freedom of maneuver. The level of unionization is high, particularly in the public sector and in the large private organizations. British trade unions also have a highly developed system of elected shop stewards who are involved in collective bargaining, sometimes on the national as well as local level. Industrial relations in Britain are characterized by an almost complete lack of legal or state intervention. Trade unions have traditionally favored the "voluntary" approach, with the law providing only a corset of basic rights. As an influential academic, Professor Otto Kahn Freund, has pointed out, there is perhaps no major country in the world in which the law has played a less significant role in the shaping of industrial relations than in Great Britain, and in which today the legal profession has less to do with industrial relations. The Industrial Relations Act of 1971 set out to change this state of affairs, failed disastrously and was repealed in 1974. The Employment Act of 1980 introduced by the present right-wing Conservative government is a new attempt to introduce the force of law into industrial relations, and no doubt it will meet the same fate.

In contrast, the trade unions of continental Europe, many of which were restructured after the war, tend to fall into several confederations, often divided on ideological and religious lines (as in France). Collective bargaining usually takes place at industry rather than plant level, although there are moves to change this. The conduct of industrial relations has a much greater legal content than in Britain. In part this derives from a cultural tradition in which the state has a long-standing concern for the social welfare of the citizen which predates his status as a wage earner. In part, too, it reflects the inability of the trade unions to settle issues by their own collective strength. In Scandinavian countries, however, an extremely high degree of unionization is coupled with extensive legal back-up to the practice of industrial relations.

Works council legislation, for example, exists in one form or another in most continental European countries. In some works councils the employer sits in the chair—a provision which undermines their independence and authority. In general, works councils possess limited powers of consultation, sometimes amounting to a temporary veto on layoffs and dismissals, some voice in hiring, a say in the formulation of work rules, and the authority to supervise the application of legally obligatory safety regulations and those aspects of the union agreement which have validity at plant level. In France the works councils often administer large and important social funds that sustain canteens and recreational facilities. In terms of power and influence, however, the German works councils are the most important.

In most cases their constitution gives them consultative functions in regard to the management of the enterprise. These provisions have remained a dead letter. Experience suggests that without independent union organization the works councils are unable to carry out effectively even the limited tasks allotted to them by the law. In Britain separate staff consultative bodies of this nature have always been opposed by the trade unions and they do not operate with any significance in British industrial relations.

Forms of Worker Participation

Worker Directors

As mentioned earlier, legal provision for worker directors exists in large number of countries in continental Europe, and the EEC commission has also put forward proposals for worker directors. The existing systems vary appreciably from one country to another, one main area of difference being whether the scheme is based on a unitary board (as in Denmark) or a two-tier board (as in Germany, where one board is concerned with day-to-day management, the other with overall policy-making). Other differences include the proportion of worker directors (a majority in Yugoslavia, a form of parity in Germany, two representatives in Sweden); how the worker directors are elected (by the trade unions in Sweden, by the works councils in France, by the whole work force in Germany); whether they have voting rights or whether they are merely observers (as in France); who is eligible for election; what types of companies are affected; and so on.

Probably the most advanced system of worker directors is the West German, which generally serves as a model for other countries. In fact, there are three different systems in operation in Germany, deriving from three different laws. All three systems are based on a two-tier board structure. Workers' direct representation and joint-decision rights relate to supervisory boards only. Workers have no direct presence on the management board, although all three participation systems provide for management board members to be appointed by majority vote of the supervisory board and one system gives workers veto powers over the appointment of a "labor director" to the management board.

The most modest of the three systems dates from a 1952 law that applies to all joint stock or limited liability companies employing between 500 and 2,000 workers. Such companies must assign one-third of the seats on the supervisory board to workers' representatives who are elected by all the work force. Both blue-collar and white-collar workers must be represented, and if more than half the work force is female there must be at least one female worker director. All worker directors have the same rights and duties as other board members. This system gives workers influence at board level, but little real authority since the share-holders' representatives have a built-in majority.

Once a company passes the 2,000 worker threshold the provi-sions of the 1976 Co-determination Act apply. The act requires equal worker and shareholder representation in numerical terms on the supervisory board. In companies with between 2,000 and 10,000 workers the board must have six workers' and six share-holders' representatives, and in companies with a workforce of 10,000 to 20,000 the board must consist of eight representatives from each side. Workers' representatives are drawn both from trade union ranks and from workers in the company, with elec-tions on the basis of proportional representation. This act gives workers considerable influence at the board level, but not ulti-mate authority, since the chairman of the board, who has the deciding vote, is a shareholders' representative. The supervisory boards are empowered to elect the members of the management board on the basis of a two-thirds majority vote, but in the event of a stalemate after a second vote the Chairman's deciding vote comes into play on a simple majority basis.

Special provisions for board-level participation in the coal, iron and steel industries derive from the Co-management Law of 1951 and its 1956 amendment. These provisions are the strongest in terms of the rights and authority they give to work-ers' representatives at board level. The provisions apply to all limited liability companies with a work force of more than 1,000 whose operations are predominantly concerned with the produc-tion of coal, iron or steel. The supervisory boards of such com-panies must consist of eleven members: five shareholders' repre-sentatives, five workers' representatives and a "neutral" eleventh person to be elected by both sides. In some larger companies the board size is fifteen or twenty-one, made up on the same basis. This system involves co-determination or joint decision-making in a much fuller sense, with the deciding vote in the hands of an agreed "independent." Supervisory boards constituted under the 1951 legislation are empowered to elect the members of the management board on a simple majority basis. This applies to all management board positions with one notable exception—the post of "labor director." No-one can be appointed to or dismissed from this post without the consent of the majority of workers' representatives on the supervisory board. This means that workers have some direct influence over the make-up of the management board team and can ensure the appointment of at least one member of their choice to the board that is responsible for personnel and labor relations policy on a day-to-day basis. Not surprisingly, there have been important controversies over individuals between the two sides.

In an interesting new development German unions have elected the general secretaries of the International Metalworkers and the International Chemical Workers to the supervisory boards of two large West German companies. They are neither West German citizens nor members of West German unions. They are there purely in their capacity as international representatives.

Europe has seen a considerable renewal of interest in the idea of worker directors. In 1973 Sweden began a three-year experiment with employee directors on company boards; the program proved successful and was renewed in 1976. Industrialists admitted that despite their initial doubts, the system had led to a better understanding between labor and management. The trade unions emphasized that their aims in putting workers on the board had been modest. They had sought insight into the workings of the board and more financial information about the company, and had achieved both aims. They had no illusions about the influence that could be wielded at board level when the employee representatives were in a minority, but they felt that their position in collective bargaining was strengthened by the insight into the company's affairs that board level representation gave them. The trade unions in banking, it is worth noting, have also taken a deep interest in investment policies.

In France, on the other hand, recent proposals to increase worker participation at the board level have been rejected by both employers and trade unions. Legislation dating from 1945 provides that public companies employing fifty persons or more must allow two delegates from the works council to participate in a consultative status in all meetings of the board of directors or supervisory board. Since 1972 the number of employee repre-

sentatives has been increased to four in enterprises employing at
least twenty-five supervisory and technical staff. In state-owned
enterprises employee representatives occupy one-third of the
seats on the board of directors and have the same rights and
obligations as the other board members. In the private sector
these provisions do not apply. In 1975, however, the Sudreau
committee proposed board-level representation in all enterprises
employing 2,000 or more, the provisions being voluntary in
smaller enterprises. Employees were to comprise one-third of the
members of the supervisory board in a two-tier system, with the
supervisory board being empowered to appoint and dismiss
members of the management board. These proposals were rejected by both sides.

In 1975 the British Labour government set up a Committee
of Inquiry into Industrial Democracy under the chairmanship of
Lord Bullock. Known as the Bullock committee, its task was "to
advise on questions relating to representation at board level in the
private sector." The committee's report, published in January
1977, concluded that the time was right for legislation to allow
employee directors on the boards of major companies. Its main
recommendations were as follows:

(i) Trade union representation on the board of directors in
companies with more than 2,000 workers;

(ii) An equal number of seats on the board for worker and
shareholder representatives, with these two groups
jointly appointing an "independent" and smaller third
group. This is known as the 2x + y formula;

(iii) Where a ballot of all employees shows a majority in favor
of worker directors, these should be appointed solely
through trade-union channels. Shop stewards would be
key figures in a system of board-level representation;

(iv) A reform of company law obliging directors to act in the
best interests of employees as well as shareholders;

(v) Multinational companies to be included in the new system
of worker directors—with modifications;

(vi) The creation of an industrial democracy commission to
advise on the new legislation and to issue codes of practice.

A main concern expressed by some unions in giving evidence
before the Bullock committee was that board-level representation

would conflict with the basic trade union activity of collective bargaining. The Bullock report disagreed, pointing out that both collective bargaining and employee directors workers' representatives share the same objective: "to enable employees to participate in decision-making in the enterprise in which they work." According to the report:

> There need not be any incompatibility between extensions to industrial democracy based on the natural development of existing forms of joint regulation below the board and a parallel extension of industrial democracy based on legislation providing for employee representation on boards. Indeed, representation at board level may be the guarantee and catalyst for effective participation at lower levels.[1]

It is clear, at any rate, that participatory schemes which do not go right to the top—that is, which do not give employees access to real decision-making—are mere illusions of participation. The Bullock Report concluded that "the crucial test which alone will carry conviction and create a willingness to share responsibility is an acknowledgement of the right of representatives of the employees, if they ask for it, to share in the strategic decisions taken by the board."[2] The committee also decided that effective labor representation could proceed only through existing trade union organizations: ". . . we do not see how or why we should make special provision for those who have chosen not to join a trade union and who are thus unable to speak with a collective voice."[3]

The Bullock Report was met with hostility from the employers and mixed feelings from the trade unions. The Labour government produced a White Paper on industrial democracy which somewhat diluted the Bullock recommendations. In any case, no legislation resulted; the Conservatives, who have no commitment to industrial democracy, came into office in 1979.

Although the development of board level representation in the private sector remains a matter for debate, recent years have seen a number of experiments in industrial democracy in publicly owned companies. One of the most advanced was a two-year experiment in the postal service which began in January 1978, but which was not renewed under the Conservative government. This experiment owed much to the Bullock recommendations. The board was comprised of seven management members, seven trade union members and five independents. It also included full-time trade union officers who would have been excluded by the Bullock recommendations because they were not employees of the postal service. The experiment was monitored by a group of sociologists who will publish their results in due course.

In accordance with legislation, both Labour and Conservative governments have appointed trade union officers to public boards on their personal merits.

There have been appointees to trading corporations such as British Gas, British Airways, financial institutions such as the Bank of England, regional development agencies and the National Enterprise Board (although the three union NEB appointees have now resigned in protest against current government policies). There are also union general secretaries who are directors of exemplary publicly owned enterprises, such as the United Kingdom Atomic Energy Authority, the National Research Development Corporation and the British National Oil Corporation (the author has served on the last two boards). In addition, a union general secretary is a government director of British Petroleum under the special constitution of that company. This system has reflected the postwar "tripartite" approach (government, unions and employers).

Other Roads to Industrial Democracy

In spite of the recent emphasis on worker participation through worker directors, this system is not the only way to democratize the workplace. The Bullock committee emphasized that worker directors should not be introduced to replace other forms of participation; but rather in order to strengthen participation at all levels. This view was reiterated during the 1977 Trades Union Congress. In Sweden, where the three-year experiment with worker directors has been judged a success, the trade unions stress that board-level representation must be seen as only one element of a broader co-determination system. And in France the Sudreau proposals for worker directors were rejected by the trade unions as an unsatisfactory response to their claims regarding trade union rights within the enterprise.

The Extension of Collective Bargaining

In 1973 a major inquiry carried out in Great Britain on behalf of the Department of Employment identified twenty-eight issues subject to bargaining between unions and management. These fell into five broad categories: wages, working conditions, hours of work, discipline and employment. These are the traditional areas of collective bargaining. None of them was ever conceded without a fight, and only in recent times has collective bargaining over the full range of these areas become anything like a well-established practice. What is clear is that the only limit to collective bargaining is the strength or weakness of the trade union movement.

There are calls throughout Europe to strengthen and extend collective bargaining. A 1977 Swedish law on co-determination extends the right of bargaining to all matters arising between employer and employees. Because of this strengthening of collective bargaining, the works councils have largely been abolished. Collective bargaining in Great Britain has been extended in a variety of areas; these are examined below.

Management of Pension Funds

Money invested in pension schemes is really deferred salary. Therefore it is entirely reasonable that the trade unions responsible for negotiating salaries should also be involved in the management of the money invested and in the disbursement of benefits. A Labour government White Paper recommended that employees participate in the running of occupational pension schemes through the agency of trade unions, with the right to nominate 50 percent of the membership of any controlling body or bodies specified in legislation. This proposal led to a storm of protest from employers who feared that it would strengthen trade union organization and lift the veil of secrecy surrounding pensions and pension fund investment. In the absence of any subsequent legislation, trade unions are seeking, with some success, to establish the principle of 50 percent representation through collective bargaining.

Equal Opportunities

In 1975 the TUC called for a determined effort to include equal opportunities clauses in all collective agreements. The recommended clause began:

> The parties of this agreement are committed to the development of positive policies to promote equal opportunities in employment regardless of workers' sex, marital status, creed,

colour, race or ethnic origins. This principle will apply in respect of all conditions of work including pay, hours of work, holiday entitlement, overtime and shift work, work allocation, guaranteed earnings, sick pay, pensions, recruitment, training, promotion and redundancy.[4]

Health and Safety

The Health and Safety at Work Act of 1974 and the appointment of workers' safety representatives and safety committees have opened up new possibilities for collective bargaining in Great Britain, encouraging the trade unions to fight more actively for safe working conditions and for the recognition of industrial diseases. In continental Europe health and safety committees usually operate within the works council system.

Reduction in Working Time

The combination of highly capital intensive industry and the economic recession in Europe, accompanied by high levels of unemployment, has encouraged the trade unions throughout Europe to work for a reduction in hours and days spent at work, the introduction of systems of work-sharing, and a more flexible approach to retirement.

Product Choice

The trade union movement has recently become more concerned with the social effects of the products it helps make. Groups of shop stewards in England have formulated alternative corporate plans for developing new products which meet manifest social needs. The most well known is the Lucas Corporate Plan. Lucas Aerospace is Europe's largest designer and manufacturer of aircraft systems and equipment. The Lucas shop stewards' proposals, which formed an integral part of the company's long-term strategy for protecting jobs, involved the consideraton of 150 alternative products for Lucas, a number of which were included because they would be socially useful to the community at large. These included medical equipment and alternative energy systems.

Disclosure of Information

Participation in decision-making and the achievement of industrial democracy can only become a reality if trade unions have access to information. The monopoly of knowledge—one of the most powerful weapons that management has at its disposal—is now being challenged by trade unions all over Europe. In Britain, trade unions have won the right, under the Employment Protection Act, to information about pay and benefits, conditions of service, manpower, performance as well as other basic financial data. New forms of collective agreements have emerged which provide for the regular disclosure of information to trade unions; these designate the type of information involved, and the frequency and level of disclosure. On the whole, however, employer resistance has obstructed the working of the Employment Protection Act; it is hard to evaluate its results, but they have not been significant.

Some disclosure of information is provided for in other European countries by the "social balance sheet" system. In France, for example, 1977 law obliges all French employers with at least 300 workers to submit annual social balance sheets, covering the last three years of activity, to the appropriate works council on a range of topics of interest to workers, including employment, pay and related costs, health and safety protection, other conditions of work, training and industrial relations. Worker directors (in those countries which have them) have been very successful in improving access to company information. Indeed, the access to information provided by board level representation was one of the main considerations of the British trade unions in their response to the Bullock report.

Perhaps the most far-reaching provisions for disclosure of information occur in Scandinavia. In Sweden, for example, the new law on co-determination makes it the duty of the employer to keep the trade union representatives informed of the financial and production aspects of the business as well as the principles on which personnel policy is based. The trade unions are also entitled to examine accounts and other documents to the extent necessary to safeguard their members' interests. In some cases unions have the right to nominate a "social" auditor, a person who examines the functioning of an enterprise in financial, employment, social, and environmental terms.

Although there are still many weaknesses in the current disclosure of information provisions in Europe, they are an important step forward in industrial relations. The call to "open the books" is one of the oldest trade union demands. Indeed, disclosure of information can be seen as the key to future developments in industrial democracy.

Technological Change

The most recent stimulus to worker participation has come from the "new technology" based on the microprocessor. Because its implementation is capable of causing workplace changes of a very radical nature, the trade unions are becoming increasingly aware that its introduction and application must be controlled. The Scandinavian unions have taken the lead in this respect.

The Norwegian Federation of Trade Unions and the Norwegian Employers Confederation have concluded a voluntary general agreement on the development and use of computer-based systems. The agreement states that all such systems must be evaluated from social as well as technical and economic standpoints. The Norwegian trade unions have also designed an educational program for union representatives. Its purpose is not to produce experts in data processing, but to help the unions understand how microprocessors will affect their work and their lives.

Using the Norwegian experience as their starting point, Sweden and Denmark are developing similar programs. In Britain the TUC has recommended that trade unions negotiate technology agreements to provide for the joint evaluation and determination of technological change. To ensure their effectiveness, technology agreements must begin with a status quo clause and also provide for:

(i) early and regular information about proposed changes;
(ii) complete information in a comprehensible form, together with access to documentation;
(iii) regular consultative meetings with the right to take any issue through bargaining procedure;
(iv) the right to reopen negotiations on existing agreements if affected by technological change;
(v) the election of technology representatives with full rights to training, time off with pay, reporting back etc.
(vi) the involvement of all those affected by particular proposed changes in the preliminary project work.[5]

These recommendations owe much to the Norwegian example and were broadly embraced by the employer's central organization in mid–1980; the member firms, however, repudiated this decision. Accordingly, the TUC decided to proceed unilaterally, and a number of technology agreements have already been successfully negotiated. Nonetheless it would be better if such agreements were obligated by law. A model for such legislation exists in Sweden, which passed a law in 1977 that requires an employer to negotiate with the trade unions before deciding on important changes at the workplace. The employer must also negotiate on any other matter if requested to by a trade union with which he has a collective agreement. The law also provides for disclosure of information to the trade unions and gives trade unions a preferred position in interpreting the joint agreements with the employer.

A comparable act in Norway provides that "the employees and their elected union representatives shall be kept informed about the systems employed for planning and effecting the work, and about planned changes in such systems. They shall be given the training necessary to enable them to learn these systems, and they shall take part in planning them."[6]

Planning Agreements

A planning agreements system for the United Kingdom was first recommended in 1973 by the Labour party, which modeled it largely on the systems already in operation in France, Belgium, and Italy. The essence of a planning agreement is a deal negotiated between a large firm and the government with the involvement of the trade unions, setting out what the firm will do to help the government meet clearly defined policy objectives. The planning agreements would fulfill the following goals:

    (i) to receive current information on a regular basis from all companies within the system, concerning both past performance and advance programs;

    (ii) to use this information to help the government identify and achieve its planning objectives and to plan for the redistribution of resources needed to meet those objectives;

    (iii) to obtain the explicit agreement of firms within the system that they will help the government meet policy objectives;

(iv) to provide for the regular revision of those agreements in the light of experience and progress;

(v) to provide a basis for channelling selective government assistance directly to those firms which agree to help meet the nation's planning objectives, since far too often companies receive public money without having to be accountable for what they do with it;

(vi) to provide a systematic basis for making large companies accountable for their actions, if necessary by using the powers of public purchasing and other methods of persuasion;

(vii) to ensure the involvement of the trade union movement in the negotiation and operation of planning agreements.

Increased information about industry would help the government plan for the future, especially as regards regional policy, import substitution, supply difficulties, and so forth. For the trade unions, planning agreements would mean increased information about the company, an opportunity to look at its problems and future prospects, and a chance to talk about all the issues affecting its performance. Only one major British company (Chrysler, which is now part of French-owned Talbot) signed a planning agreement as part of a government financial aid package. The agreement did not survive the strain of the French take-over, although a government-nominated director, who is a trade union general secretary, survives on the United Kingdom board.

In the future, collective bargaining will have a more integral role both as regards planning agreements and the process of planning in general. Ways are now being considered, through legislative support and the development of multiunion representation, how to provide an explicit role for collective bargaining in formulating and executing planning decisions. Such agreements would not replace direct board representation for trade unionists, however, but serve as a complementary provision appropriate in some industries.

Conclusion

The demand for increased worker participation is common throughout Europe, though the objectives and experiences of workers in different countries have varied. This demand is wholly natural since an absence of participation is incompatible with a truly democratic society.

Trade union structure and traditional patterns of industrial relations have shaped the different forms of worker participation. In the United Kingdom the combination of relatively strong heterogeneous unions and a voluntarist tradition has led to an emphasis on collective bargaining and a resistance to the legislative provisions for worker directors and works councils which predominate in the other major countries. In the future, increased resort to legislation to support collective bargaining rights, the development of forms of joint-union representation and, to a lesser extent, increased provision for worker directors will serve to lessen this contrast. The activities of both the EEC Commission and the ETUC (European Trade Union Confederation) will be influential on future development.

The structural problems faced by industry, new technology, the changing pattern of "ownership" and new political initiatives will all be acting as catalysts toward further development of worker participation. While many different routes will be explored—including increased provision for worker directors, enhanced statutory rights to information and consultation, the provision for increased worker inputs into industrial planning processes—the essential purpose underlying them all is the democratization of industry.

Notes

1. Committee of Enquiry on Industrial Democracy, *Report* (HMSO: London, 1977).
2. Ibid.
3. Ibid.
4. British Trades Union Congress, *Annual Report*, 1975.
5. British Trades Union Congress, *Report on Employment and Technology*, 1979.
6. Norway, *Worker Protection and Working Environment Act* (Oslo: Directorate of Labor Inspection).

9

Workplace Democracy in Sweden

Results, Failures, and Hopes

ANNA-GRETA LEIJON

Anna-Greta Leijon is a Social Democratic party (SAP) member of the Swedish parliament. She was Minister of Labor and Employment in the Palme government from 1973 to 1976.

In the following essay she offers a detailed analysis of the Co-determination Act of 1977, as well as of previous legislation leading to that monumental act—probably the most radical in Western Europe. She details the three levels of decision-making in which Swedish workers may now participate—work organization (shopfloor matters), administration of the company (planning, personnel policy), and management (seats on the board of directors). Leijon concludes on a pessimistic note, observing that the Co-determination Act coincided with the economic recession of the 1970s, thereby undercutting its potential. She believes the establishment of wage-earner investment funds is now necessary to make the Co-determination Act live up to the Swedish labor movement's high expectations for increased worker control.

WORKPLACE DEMOCRACY IN SWEDEN:
Results, Failures, and Hopes

Anna-Greta Leijon

The controversial issues of profit sharing, industrial and economic democracy, the influence exerted by employees on capital, and co-determination have been debated in the majority of Western European countries during the postwar era, and perhaps above all during the 1950s and 1960s. A large number of proposals have been put forward, with the result that co-determination, joint influence and economic democracy now exist in a wide variety of forms throughout Europe. Wim Kok, chairman of the European Confederation of Trade Unions and also chairman of the Dutch Labor Confederation observed last autumn at a seminar in Stockholm that despite variations in different countries, the tendency is clear: "The European worker wants co-determination, not only outside enterprise but inside it as well."

So far, however, although the European trade union movement has formulated goals of joint influence and co-determination, it has not designed practical ways and means for their attainment. There have been serious disagreements about strategy. Some trade union organizations feel that workers' influence should not be exercised through management bodies but rather through the trade unions or through other workers' agencies.

It seems fair to say that disparate opinions have converged of late. It is being increasingly acknowledged that greater influence cannot be achieved without a certain degree of joint responsibility. This entails participation on company committees accompanied by the responsibility to help formulate and supervise company policy at *all* levels in an enterprise.

This essay is concerned with Swedish labor legislation and above all with the Co-determination Act. It will prove helpful to begin with a brief sketch of Swedish labor history, however, in order to suggest the context from which this legislation emerged.

Balance of Power on the Employers' Terms

The Industrial Revolution came quite late to Sweden. Conflicts between workers and employers were often large and serious, and workers encountered great difficulty in building labor organizations. It was only at the beginning of this century that the workers secured the right to form trade unions without interference from employers. In order to obtain this right, the workers were forced to allow employers the right to organize work and to hire and dismiss workers as they pleased.

In December 1906 an agreement, sometimes called the December Compromise, between the Swedish Confederation of Trade Unions (LO) and the Swedish Employers' Confederation (SAF) confirmed this state of affairs and profoundly influenced the subsequent development of labor relations in Sweden. The December Compromise of 1906 denied the trade union organizations influence at workplaces, but efficient organization and close cooperation with the Social Democratic party nonetheless made it possible for the trade-union organizations to play an important role in Swedish society. More labor legislation followed during the 1920s and 1930s. The most important agreement, concluded in 1938, is commonly referred to as the Saltsjöbaden Agreement, after the place near Stockholm where it was signed. This agreement established the rules of collective bargaining and the right and status of third parties in connection with industrial disputes. This main agreement from 1938 has played a very important part in Swedish labor relations.

Full Employment and Democracy as Union Policy

Full employment became a central policy aim of the party and the trade union movement from the 1930s onwards. The trade unions fought hard for its acceptance, and they committed their organizational strength and their political influence to its accomplishment.

Sweden has a very high rate of trade union membership. LO, the largest group of trade unions, represents more than two million workers in private enterprise and the public sector. No less than 90 percent of employees in these categories belong to LO. The union membership rate of salaried employees is somewhat lower, but is still about 80 percent. This means, of course, that the trade unions are much stronger in all respects than in countries where a large proportion of employees are not organized. One should remember, however that employers are also well organized in Sweden. Whereas the trade-union organizations have devoted most of their efforts to improve wages and working conditions, to secure full employment and to work actively for social reform, the employers have devoted much of their effort to preserve the power gains they made in the important December Compromise of 1906 and which were consolidated in the 1930 Saltsjöbaden Agreement.

The demand for industrial democracy has been pressed at various times, but the real campaign for reform did not start until the 1970s. Both LO and TCO (the Swedish Central Organization of Salaried Employees) raised the question of the democratization of working life during the first half of the 1960s, mainly with reference to various forms of workplace consultation. This led to an agreement on joint councils. But the salaried workers' movement and LO quite soon found that they wanted more extensive influence than the consultative rules of the joint councils agreement afforded, for these rules presupposed (as before) that it was the employer's prerogative to direct and allocate work and to hire and dismiss job applicants.

The trade unions began to press demands for influence at all decision-making levels. They argued that democracy should be the guiding principle of all activities in the community. Moreover, they maintained that democracy should be employed as a means for improving the working conditions of employees. This debate elicited a positive, if cautious response from employers, who had economic reasons of their own for raising these questions. During the late 1960s it had become increasingly difficult for them to recruit and retain employees for industrial work. Not only in Sweden but in large parts of the Western world, developments pointed to a gulf between the working conditions entailed by modern technology and the demands made by an increasingly well-educated corps of job applicants.

The reform of working life centered first on occupational safety and health. And there were many reasons for this. There was a strongly felt need for improvements to occupational safety and health, and the trade unions therefore found it very easy indeed to activate their members on the subject. Also, it was a safe bet that employers' resistance to worker influence would be less in this area than in most others.

Concern with workers' physical protection was gradually superseded by concern with the occupational environment, which came to include the social and psychological conditions at the workplace. Questions concerning work organization, solitary work, and the selection of tools and machines became important aspects of the occupational environment, and in this way the workers began to nibble at the edges of important areas hitherto sacrosanct to employers.

Workers' influence may take various forms, but there are essentially three modes of participation in decision-making: negotiation, representation in joint bodies, and self-determination. During the 1960s Sweden embarked on experimental activities aimed at the democratization of working life and the practical testing of different forms of co-determination. The main focus of these activities was on the so-called autonomous groups and joint decision-making groups. The parties were supported in part by state subsidies; ideas were to a great extent derived from the autonomous groups in Norway.

In the early 1970s, however, after some years of bipartite experimentation within both LO and TCO, the various organizations presented their findings. Both LO and TCO determined to work for worker influence through negotiations. They requested political support for legislation conferring influence far in excess of what the employers were prepared to concede at the negotiating table. The employers for their part dug in their heels concerning managerial decisions in enterprise. But one must admit that they showed interest in looking for new solutions relating to work organization.

1974–76: An Intensive Period of Reform

The first half of the 1970s saw a period of government inquiries followed by a rapid series of enactments concerning job security, educational leave, worker directors, the occupational environment, the status of shop stewards and co-determination. The Security of Employment Act, passed in 1974, did away with the liberty of employers to dismiss workers at will, stipulating that there must be objective grounds for dismissal. This act also stipulates a minimum of one month's notice. A person employed for six months and over a certain age is entitled to a longer period of notice. For example, a worker aged forty-five or over is entitled to six months' notice.

The Shop Stewards Act, also passed in 1974, stipulates that trade union activities at the workplace are in the interests of the enterprise, and that shop stewards are therefore entitled to leave of absence. Moreover, if leave of absence is occasioned by trade union activities at the workplace, the enterprise must bear the cost entailed by the shop steward, which means that the shop steward is entitled to retain his normal pay and other benefits.

The legislation enacted between 1974 and 1976 does not represent a sudden change of course in Swedish labor relations. On the contrary, the postwar era saw one reform after another enacted and implemented.

Legislation establishing two weeks' holiday had been passed in 1938. Statutory holidays were gradually increased to four weeks and then, in 1977, to five weeks. Working hours had totalled forty-eight hours per week since 1919, but in 1957 they were reduced to forty-five hours per week. Since then the working week has been reduced by an hour or so every year, until in 1970 it reached forty hours. Compulsory health insurance was introduced, providing benefits proportional to loss of earnings. And a general supplementary pensions scheme (ATP) was introduced in 1959.

This process of reform presents a consistent pattern. Holidays, shorter working hours, sickness benefits and pensions were benefits that salaried employees at the great majority of firms had secured by collective agreement, but they were now made universal. The 1974 Security of Employment Act, with its rules concerning periods of notice and its restriction of the right of employers to lay off workers without pay, really marked the final stage in a series of reforms, all of which were aimed at placing manual workers on an equal footing with white collar and executive workers.

The Co-determination Act

The cornerstone of modern Swedish labor legislation is the Co-determination Act, which came into force early in 1977. The act is a mixture of old and new. Some of its provisions have survived intact from the 1928 Collective Agreements Act, while its provisions concerning the right of association come from the 1936 Collective Bargaining Act, and its provisions concerning conciliation from an act passed in 1920.

What is new about the Co-determination Act is the provision it makes concerning various forms of co-determination. First and foremost, an employer is required to negotiate with the trade union organizations before making extensive alterations. The rules giving the trade union organization priority of interpretation in disputes concerning the duties of the individual worker are also vitally important. So too is the question of a veto in certain cases concerning the placement of jobs with contractors. The act also contains a general declaration to the effect that agreements are to be concluded concerning powers of co-determination for employees in matters relating to the conclusion and termination of a contract of service and the direction and allocation of work; these are areas which the employers were formerly anxious to retain as their prerogative in keeping with the 1906 December Compromise and the 1938 Saltsjöbaden Agreement.

The process leading to the Co-determination Act began with the government's appointment of a labor legislation committee in late 1971. The years immediately preceding had been characterized by heavy economic expansion; there had been much discussion concerning the difficulties of recruiting personnel for industrial employment, and there was a general spirit of optimism in economic life and in the labor market.

This situation had changed a great deal by the time the Co-determination Act came into force six years later. Unemployment and great economic difficulties predominated, and the country had acquired a nonsocialist government. As mentioned earlier, the Co-determination Act envisaged that the parties would conclude agreements on co-determination. This has in fact happened, but with one important exception. No such agreement has been concluded between the employers' confederation and LO and PTK (the Federation of Salaried Employees in Industry and Services). Negotiations on this subject have broken down twice, in 1978 and 1980. In 1978 the employers' confederation attempted to negotiate a waiver of trade union rights, including priority of interpretation. In the second round of talks the points at dispute in 1978 had to all intents and purposes been settled, but the employers then pressed hard for different rules for large and small enterprises. In addition, there were other questions on which the employers were adamant. The unions felt that the employers were more concerned with adopting a political stance than with seeking an agreement.

The joint council agreements (which guided the 1960s experiments in joint decision-making) had been cancelled at the end of 1976, just before the Co-determination Act came into force, and the central union organizations and federations called on their local branches to refrain from participation in joint bodies and to rely on negotiations under the Co-determination Act instead. Most did just that, but at some workplaces the earlier routines for employer-employee contacts have been retained even though there no longer exists any agreement governing these activities. The two sides have simply carried on in the accustomed manner pending a co-determination agreement.

Co-determination Agreements

Central co-determination agreements can be found throughout the public sector and in the cooperative sector of the labor market. The co-determination agreement for national government authorities defines three types of influence. The first of these comprises negotiations under the Co-determination Act.

The second implies that the employer must obtain union approval before making a decision; in other words, the trade unions have a kind of veto. And the third implies that the union should arrive at its decisions after negotiations with the national authority, which might be termed a form of union self-determination. Thus the agreement makes it possible for the parties to enter into local accords for the implementation of one of these three forms of co-determination. Union powers of veto may be exercised in decisions concerning the use of psychological suitability tests, planning discussions and dismissal interviews. Union self-determination after negotiations can be applied to decisions concerning certain organizational matters and the induction of new employees, and to decisions concerning workplace meetings. Thus powers of veto and self-determination are confined to very limited areas.

Accordingly, the main emphasis of the agreement in the cooperative sector and the agreement with the state enterprises is on co-determination by negotiation.

Employers on the whole prefer a system that will be as fast and straightforward as possible and that entails a minimum of alteration to existing decision-making routines, as well as involving a minimum of meetings. For their part, the unions want to avoid participating in decisions they cannot influence. They want a system that will enable their members to see what the union line is and what the management has decided that might conflict with the will of the union. They do not want to be party to decisions they do not support, and they want to avoid a vague role in a decision-making process where it is not clear who thinks what and who decides what.

A short review of co-determination at different levels within the enterprise may prove helpful. Three such levels can be distinguished. The first is the organization, direction and allocation of work. The second can be termed administration. And the third level comprises issues of management.

Co-determination Regarding Work Organization

The issue of work organization has a vital bearing on the development of co-determination. Employers and trade-union organizations have agreed that the most important element in co-determination is the individual's ability to exert more influence on matters of everyday relevance. The demand for a democratization of work organization is largely an indictment of the type of production organization which has predominated during the twentieth century, namely Taylorism, fragmentation, detailed control and supervision. The Co-determination Act contains no specific provisions concerning how work should be organized, but it clearly states that work organization *ought* to be a subject of negotiation. Moreover, the act includes several rules intended to support the conclusion of such agreements. There are also other laws, quite separate from the Co-determination Act, that make stipulations of a more general nature concerning qualities that are desirable in the occupational environment.

The Co-determination Act also lays down rules concerning the right of the trade union organization in disputes concerning duties covered by an agreement. This means, for example, that in a disagreement concerning the nature of an employee's duty or how he performs it, the employer must accept the union's interpretation pending a determination of the matter by the Labor Court. Priority of interpretation also applies to negotiations concerning transfers to other duties. This rule provides unions with excellent opportunities to assert their interests.

At the deadlocked negotiations for a co-determination agreement in the private sector, the LO and PTK union organizations put forward several demands for the right of employees to decide matters of work organization. These included the right of unions to request work organization on a group basis, to decide the size and composition of the group and the allocation of work, and to control work planning and dissemination of information within the group. Unions have also demanded the power to veto changes affecting work organization. Other demands are that unions decide criteria for remuneration and also the distribution of working hours and holidays.

The two sides remain far apart from each other in some of these matters.

Where agreements have been reached, unions have obtained improvements in matters of work organization. In the state sector, for example, parties at the local level can conclude agreements concerning rationalization measures and other changes in work organization. But, there is still no central co-determination agreement which limits the traditional superiority of the employer to determine work organization.

There is an interesting work organization agreement in a small engineering firm (about 300 employees) in the Stockholm area. This agreement originally applied to only one of the firm's departments, but similar agreements were subsequently included for others. The agreement governs the right of employees within the group to make their own decisions concerning such matters as job allocation, temporary overtime, short-term leave of absence and planning. The process began with local studies and has been built up step by step. The local union committee kept the issue alive and gradually increased its powers and the activity of its members. Cooperation was established with the associations of salaried employees, and eventually developments were thus codified in agreements with the employer. This can be termed a happy example of what LO wishes to achieve through co-determination.

Despite a few exceptions, however, the trade-union organizations have not been successful in making progress by means of negotiations. It is clear that employers are reluctant to relinquish their traditional control of the workplace. Often the greatest opportunities for improvements follow major investments that involve the construction of new facilities, alterations to existing ones or the purchase of machinery.

The discussion of work organization has generally centered on industrial jobs, above all monotonous assembly jobs. But organizational questions are no less relevant in other areas. In nursing and care, for instance, group therapy has gained increasing currency. Group routines in cleaning, repair, and maintenance work have also been introduced by the unions.

Overall, reports on the implementation of the Co-determination Act suggest only meager developments in the area of work organization. This may reflect actual conditions. The low level of investments following the introduction of the act may have limited the opportunities for change. There are many indications that these issues have not yet become a subject of formal co-determination negotiations.

Co-determination in Administration

Administrative issues generally fall in between issues concerning top management and those concerning day-to-day production of goods or services. They include some aspects of planning, personnel policy and administration. The Co-determination Act requires the employer to supply the trade unions with comprehensive information in these areas. If an agreement confers powers of co-determination on employees, the union has priority of interpretation. In matters concerning the engagement of contractors, the trade unions have a veto if they have cause to believe that the contractor is guilty of improprieties concerning taxation or other laws and agreements. Moreover, the act requires employers to negotiate before embarking on any major change in operations.

It is still too early to evaluate the performance of the Co-determination Act; the evidence is incomplete. Many employers continue to offend against the provisions concerning the primary duty of negotiation, but much of this represents a lingering of old habits. Certainly the act cannot be said to have wrought any dramatic changes. Still, there has been an improvement in the information supplied to the trade union organizations. On the other hand, some union representatives believe that the view commanded by unions of personnel planning and similar matters has deteriorated following the substitution of negotiations for personnel committees. Even if true, it does not necessarily follow that employees have lost influence since the act came into force; on the whole, the opposite appears true.

The labor market reforms of the 1970s have proven harder to implement within small firms. Many of the provisions of the Co-determination Act, for example, presuppose bureaucratic procedures and written documentation commonly found only in large organizations.

Co-determination and Company Management

The management of companies in both the public and private sectors is usually divided between a board of directors and an executive management. The influence exerted by employees at management level is primarily defined in the legislation concerning board representation (through worker directors), which affects more than 8,000 firms. But the Co-determination Act is also designed to obtain greater employee input in management. The power of negotiation in this area, however, is subject to many restrictions. One important restriction concerns the public sector, in which decisions concerning goals, direction, scope and quality of activities are made by political bodies. In the private sector a corresponding exception is made for activities of a religious, scientific, artistic or ideological nature, as well as those serving a cooperative, trade unionist, political or other opinion–forming purpose. The difficulty in agreeing upon restrictions has led to an extensive debate on principles, and a special committee has been set up to deal with disputes concerning the boundary between political democracy and industrial democracy. So far, however, this committee has not been called upon to act.

The relatively widespread criticism levelled against the Co-determination Act in the course of public debate has focussed primarily on the provisions concerning management. The act simply does not give unions the power to stop management in crucial decisions dealing with closures, dismissals, relocation and so forth. Once management has discharged its obligation to inform and negotiate, it can go ahead and decide things exactly as before. On the other hand, time determines the practical influence wielded by the trade union organizations in individual cases. If management is in a hurry, the unions can exert influence by threatening to exercise its right of delay, but a management which has plenty of time can conduct negotiations both centrally and locally and then go through with its decisions according to plan.

These limitations make it clear that the Co-determination Act does not always provide effective support for the trade union organizations, but it was never the Riksdag's (Parliament's) intention to give trade union organizations the power, on the strength of the act, to solve major economic crises and the employment problems that follow in their wake.

Co-determination in Groups of Companies

Combines present a very special kind of problem. The provisions of the Co-determination Act concerning negotiations are primarily framed with reference to individual enterprises. But the 1970s saw a considerable growth in the number of conglomerates in the private sector, as a result both of company take-overs and the subdivision of enterprises. It is not uncommon for parent companies to do business through subsidiaries. Decisions by the Labor Court, however, have established that the management of a subsidiary is answerable to its trade-union counterparts for measures taken by the parent company.

The multinationals are a special instance of the problem connected with groups of companies. About 50,000 persons in Sweden are employed by foreign-owned enterprises, and more than 300,000 persons in other countries are employed by groups headquartered in Sweden. Formally speaking, the Co-determination Act only applies to employer-employee relations in Sweden, and part of the problem with foreign-owned multinationals is that local Swedish management in many cases cannot influence decisions made abroad concerning activities in Sweden. Sometimes the Swedish management is not even informed that decisions are being made elsewhere.

Unfulfilled Expectations

External circumstances have affected the course of co-determination. In times of economic expansion and rising prosperity, decisions focus on investments, enlargements, the procurement of capital and the recruitment of personnel. In times of economic decline, decisions deal with retrenchment— cutbacks and transfers, possible lay-offs and dismissals. Since 1977 Sweden has on the whole been subject to economic recession.

It is too early yet to draw firm conclusions about the Co-determination Act, but the trade unions appear to be disappointed with the outcome. The act was passed at the behest of the unions as an important part of a general overhaul of laws and regulations for the Swedish labor market. The reform process was surrounded by a great deal of political and trade-unionist debate, and expectations were pitched high. Negotiations were to provide the principal means of augmenting workers' influence. Although co-determination has probably increased as a result of the act, the results so far have fallen short of expectations. The rules which the unions value above all are those concerning information, priority of interpretation and the union veto concerning contractors. It is fair to say that employers have been able to continue as if nothing had happened. On the other hand, their apprehensions of a ballooning bureaucracy, heavier costs, and impaired efficiency have not been borne out by events.

The trade union organizations are debating the road ahead. Not long ago an LO representative closely concerned with these matters published an interesting article which posed three questions: First, is co-determination too much a matter of legislation and rules? Second, why is our understanding of co-determination improving so slowly? And third, has co-determination been forced on the defensive? The article concludes with an appeal to the entire labor movement to rally round co-determination and make it part of the trade-unionist and political struggle.

During the past year employers have levelled barrages of criticism against current labor legislation. There is no doubt that a great divide has come into being, and that the trade unions and employers are a good deal further apart today than they were at the beginning of the 1970s. Yet the unions want labor legislation to go further, and discussions are in progress concerning wage-earner funds in one form or another. These discussions are concerned with reinforcing workers' influence beyond the bounds existing co-determination agreements. The question of employee participation in the formation of capital is now the most vital economic issue both in Sweden and the other Western European democracies.

10

The Workers' Role in
Decision-Making

IRVING BLUESTONE

Irving Bluestone is the American labor movement's foremost
expert and proponent of workers' participation. A recently retired vice-president of the United Auto Workers (UAW), he is
currently a professor of labor studies at Wayne State University,
Michigan.

Bluestone begins his analysis by noting that the underdeveloped nature of the American welfare state has forced trade
unions in the United States to bargain collectively for many social
services that have been legislated in Western Europe. Thus collective bargaining, with its clear adversary roles between workers
and management, is the key to increasing workers' influence in
the quality and nature of their work life. Bluestone cautions,
however, that helping to manage the entire enterprise through
representatives on boards of directors is simply not on the American trade union agenda in the forseeable future.

THE WORKERS' ROLE IN DECISION-MAKING

Irving Bluestone

Labor-management relations in the United States have been characterized as "pragmatic": the workers have a problem and the union responds by bargaining with the employer for a solution. Or the employer acts and the union responds in order to protect the interests of the worker. Unionism's "pragmatic" approach to satisfying worker concerns is, of course, rooted in America's economic, political and social system as it evolved in the period following the Industrial Revolution.

In a real sense, unionism in the United States is a reflection of the nature of management, which has been (and in many quarters continues to be) fiercely resistant to the idea of workers organizing into unions to advance and protect their welfare. Thus unionism was born in the cradle of conflict, and the adversarial climate has colored the development of labor-management relations throughout the decades of union struggle and achievement.

Unionism in the United States has not embraced any particular social or political philosophy. It is not tied to any particular "ism." That is not to say it has no social conscience, for indeed labor is the single most persistent and enduring champion of social and economic justice. Unions, however, recognize as their

179

primary responsibility organizing the unorganized and representing the workers in collective bargaining to improve their standard of living and establish and preserve decent job conditions at the workplace. The pursuit of social policy—political and legislative goals to advance the general welfare of the total community—rides on the back of unionism's primary functions of organizing and bargaining collectively.

A manifest result of this history has been the development of a complex network of collective bargaining goals which concentrates on the problems of immediate worker concern. It has evolved into a system in which collective bargaining bears an unwieldy burden, attempting through more or less isolated negotiated settlements to satisfy social needs that are national in scope and concerning which legislated social policy is faulty or absent altogether.

Few would contest any longer that providing income maintenance during periods when a worker is involuntarily unable to work is sound social policy. It keeps bread and butter on the table; it sustains purchasing power needed to keep the wheels of production turning; it is consistent with the morality of a democratic society. Thus, it is sound social policy that a worker laid off for lack of work should receive adequate income replacement until he finds another job. Unfortunately, state-legislated unemployment benefits, which are inadequate at best, vary widely both in amount and in requirements for eligibility among the fifty states; hence it is necessary for collective bargaining to supplement income during periods of unemployment.

It is also sound social policy that a worker who is "too old to work but too young to die" should receive a lifetime income sufficient to maintain decent living standards. But social security benefits are too meager, and societal failure once again places additional burden on collective bargaining to supplement inadequate government programs. Further, it is sound social policy that a worker who is ill should receive income replacement as well as a full measure of health-care protection. Yet the burden once again, except for the elderly and the disabled, falls entirely on collective bargaining.

It could be effectively argued, moreover, that it is sound social policy for workers to receive vacation time off with pay, to rest, relax and refresh themselves. Yet collective bargaining rather than legislated requirement carries the burden of fulfilling that need. And these are only some areas of community responsibility which fall to collective bargaining because of the vacuum created by either inadequate or totally absent social legislation.

A primary principle should apply to these and other problems of national responsibility. If some citizens are forced to suffer to advance the common welfare of all citizens, then government is obligated to repair the damage. And if certain economic benefits are needed to strengthen and preserve the total community, then the total community should provide them for all the people to enjoy. They should not become the special burden of collective bargaining in the private sector, covering only those whose unions are strong enough to negotiate them, and leaving bereft or subject to management's whim those whose unions are weak or who lack union protection altogether.

In terms of material advantage to the worker—an improved standard of living and economic security—and in terms of the improvement in working conditions, American unions have made commendable progress. But vast areas of decision-making that seriously affect the welfare and security of the workers remain largely beyond their reach.

Management, by way of example, controls the decision to shut down a plant or move all or part of it to another location, often hundreds of miles away. The union bargains for severance pay, early retirement, the right of the worker to transfer with the job and to receive moving allowance, and so forth. But the worker—often with long years of service—is the victim of such a decision. He is permanently thrown out of work or, even if he is given the right to transfer with the job, he must pull up stakes, uproot himself from his community, leave family ties and friends, and begin a new life in a strange place with no assurance of permanence. Management wields the decision-making authority; the worker (and the community) dangles at the end of that decision. Similarly, management generally controls the final decision to subcontract work out or to move work about among the many facilities in a multiplant corporation. It is the worker who faces the ultimate insecurity.

These kinds of decisions impact directly upon the welfare of the worker. He has an easily recognizable stake in their immediate results. In a more remote, but equally significant way, decisions regarding products, product design, accounting procedures, marketing, purchasing, capital investment and so forth, also affect the income and job security of the worker.

Labor, for the most part, has operated under the following policy: let management manage and the workers will react to what they don't like. For example, from its birth as a union until its constitutional convention in 1980, the constitution of the United Auto Workers carried the following provision in its preamble: "The worker does not seek to usurp management's functions or ask for a place on the Board of Directors of concerns where organized." This and other clauses were deleted by action of the 1979 UAW convention delegates. Today the preamble contains, among others, the following declarations:

> The precepts of democracy require that workers through their union participate meaningfully in making decisions affecting their welfare and that of the communities in which they live.
>
> Managerial decisions have far-reaching impact upon the quality of life enjoyed by the workers, the family, the community. Management must recognize that it has basic responsibilities to advance the welfare of the workers and the whole society and not alone to the stockholders. It is essential, therefore, that the concerns of workers and of society be taken into account when basic managerial decisions are made.
>
> The structure of work established by management is designed to make of the workers an adjunct to the tool rather than its master. This, coupled with the authoritarian climate of the workplace robs the worker of his dignity as an adult human being. This belies the democratic heritage we cherish as citizens in a society rooted in democratic values.
>
> Essential to the UAW's purpose is to afford the opportunity for workers to master their work environment: to achieve not only improvement in their economic status but, of equal importance, to gain from their labors a greater measure of dignity, of self-fulfillment and self-worth.
>
> Workers must also participate meaningfully in political and legislative action because government impacts importantly on their lives and on their communities. If government is to be the means by which people achieve a humanitarian

and equitable society, it must be a responsible and account-able government.

Therefore, the UAW has the duty and responsibility to promote real and meaningful participatory democracy through its members and their families, so that free people and their institutions may be heard in the councils of govern-ment and so that officeholders are guided by principle alone.

To achieve these wholesome objectives:

- Management must accept union organization and collec-tive bargaining as an essential and constructive force in our democratic society;
- The workers must be provided a meaningful voice in maintaining a safe and healthful workplace with decent working conditions, and must enjoy secured rights, together with a satisfactory standard of living and max-imum job security;
- The workers must have a voice in their own destiny and the right to participate in making decisions that affect their lives before such decisions are made;
- The UAW must play an active role at all levels of govern-ment to protect the lives and rights of its members and their families. We must work constantly on the political and legislative problem facing the whole society;
- Union members must take seriously their responsibilities as citizens and work, through their union and individu-ally, to realize the goals of participatory democracy and responsible and accountable government.

In the past decade, labor-management relations have wit-nessed the birth pangs of new and, for the United States, novel developments. In one sense they represent the natural extension of the workers' drive to achieve industrial democracy. In another sense, they are novel departures from traditional labor-management relationships, in that workers and their repre-sentations are participating, or attempting to win the right to participate, in decisions previously understood to be purely man-agement functions.

It must be emphasized that collective bargaining in the adversarial mode will continue unabated over traditional issues such as wages and other economic benefits, working conditions and the myriad of working provisions of the labor contract. After all, the first concern of the worker—and it should be the first concern of society—is to earn a decent living and provide for his family. Food, clothes, housing and health considerations take precedence.

However, the economic system in the United States has never solved the problem of persistent unemployment (except in periods of war). Full employment is a national issue of such dimensions that it requires a national solution. Collective bargaining alone cannot solve it. However, here again, societal failure to create enough jobs compels collective bargaining to attempt to fill the vacuum. Labor demands reduction in work time as one means to create job opportunities. Since neither the political nor the economic system is providing the answer, the issue remains a hard-core collective bargaining matter. Labor is also beginning to address other problems of national scope: plant shutdowns and relocation of plants; subcontracting of work both within the country and to foreign producers; the impact of advancing technology upon job security and wages; etc., the "double standard" which favors white-collar workers over blue-collar workers. These and a host of other economic and noneconomic issues are moving into the collective bargaining arena.

Despite the intensity of the bargaining process when controversial issues are at stake, there are many subjects of mutual concern and interest which call for a joint, cooperative effort between management and labor. Some must first be pounded out in principle in traditional bargaining forays, such as the establishment of joint committees on health and safety. There are others whose inception call for reasonable parties to work together in a nonadversarial atmosphere. In this latter category we find the recent joint efforts to promote work reorganization and the meaningful involvement of the worker in the decision-making process.

Many joint programs undertaken by the union and management already exist. Citing some of these will help suggest the vast possibilities for cooperative union-management efforts in the future.

Alcoholism Rehabilitation

Alcoholism, long a festering problem, was traditionally handled by management as a matter for progressive discipline. Yet discipline could not and did not correct the alcoholic. Succeedingly severe disciplinary measures simply aggravated the illness and led to his discharge. Thus management lost the employee's training and skills; the employee lost his paycheck—and often his family—and society lost the benefit of a productive citizen. Joint alcoholism rehabilitation programs are now established which recognize that alcoholism is an illness like other illnesses. Management and union representatives with training and expertise work together assisting the alcoholic who seeks or is induced to seek help. Thousands of ill workers have thus been restored to health, to their jobs and to their families. They are once again contributors to the welfare of society.

Similar activities are developing for the problem of drug addiction. True, the cures are still uncertain. Nevertheless, workers who seek help are being provided a measure of assistance through joint cooperative union-management programs. In addition, cooperative efforts are expanding to cover a broad range of emotional and familial problems.

Orientation Programs for the Newly Hired

Joint programs to help orient new employees in their jobs is another cooperative undertaking. In such programs knowledgeable management and union representatives jointly meet with new workers and provide them with pertinent information concerning their job, the union, the company, and so on. Thus they enter upon a new and often strange world armed with some helpful knowledge concerning the workplace and the people with whom they will be thrown into contact.

Preretirement Programs

Joint preretirement programs involve not only the prospective retiree but the spouse as well. Here again instruction and pertinent information are provided jointly by management and union representatives in meetings whose agenda is designed to assist workers contemplating retirement.

Discipline

In some cases union and management are attempting to find ways to handle problems of discipline in individual workers. How successful these experiments prove remains to be seen, but it is interesting that in some instances management is willing to seek the assistance of the union in correcting the behavior of straying workers before invoking discipline. It suggests that management, at least in some places, is willing to test the theory that a willingness to help a worker resolve his personal problems can be a more effective deterrent to aberrant behavior than threats and punishment. How often have foremen come to the realization that the habitual absentee prefers disciplinary time off as the penalty; it provides more time away from the job, "sanctioned" by management!

Apprenticeship Training

Joint apprentice training programs are of long standing, with the union and management making certain that apprentices are properly selected and their training is appropriate to their trade.

Administration of Benefit Plans

Joint administration of worker benefit plans, such as pensions and health care, are also traditional to the union-management relationship. Together the parties determine the facts in any disputed situation, apply the provisions of the program and correct errors in payment or coverage. Some UAW contracts include an independent medical arbitration procedure to resolve disputes between doctors over eligibility for sickness and accident benefits or total and permanent disability. Programs that insure workers' eligibility for retirement benefits, that calculate the amount of those benefits, and that explain to prospective retirees their rights, and provide them with all the information they need, lend themselves to joint union-management cooperation.

Health and Safety

Perhaps the most significant development in cooperative effort between the union and the management is the establishment of joint health and safety committees. The worker, after all, is the first-line victim of inadequate health and safety conditions at the workplace. With the proliferation of joint committees, health and safety programs have been elevated in importance and urgency. Literally thousands of corrective actions are taken each year as a result of their findings.

Joint health and safety programs normally arise from the heat of tough collective bargaining, but once the provisions are written as part of the labor contract, their implementation becomes a matter of mutual concern and cooperation. Admittedly, this does not mean all controversy over health and safety matters disappears. But it does influence the parties to work together to remove hazards and create a safe and healthful workplace. Health and safety matters represent a unique mixture of cooperative effort on the one hand and tough controversy on the other.

The joint, cooperative programs described above are healthy developments which benefit the worker, the management and the union. They enhance labor-management relations. However, they do not involve the worker directly in the decision-making process, which is the essential next step toward improving the quality of worklife.

Participation in the decision-making process is fundamental to the democratic way of life, which is the life blood of our society. In a democratic society workers as citizens enjoy broad rights of decision-making which are denied to those living in autocratic societies. They have the right, through their vote, to determine who their leaders will be. With their vote they can also turn those same leaders out of office. As family members and residents of their community they participate in a myriad of decisions affecting their lives, the well-being of their loved ones and their neighbors and fellow citizens. In the workplace, however, they are the obeyers of orders. Suffice it to say, it is time that a social order anchored in democratic principles insures each individual at the workplace a significant measure of the dignity, self-respect, and freedom enjoyed as a citizen.

Participation in the decision-making process manifests itself in two fundamental ways: "managing the job" and "managing the enterprise." "Managing the job" is a subject receiving increasing attention on the part of both unions and management. It means affording workers the opportunity to play a meaningful role in making decisions regarding work processes, the methods and means of production, plant layout, quality of product control, job design, and so forth. These are areas from which workers have traditionally been excluded. Worker participation programs would change workers from order takers and adjuncts of their tools to decision-makers and masters of their tools.

This transformation will not be easily achieved. Nor does it spring full-blown out of the adversarial collective bargaining relationship. It requires patience, painstaking understanding and, above all, changes in attitude which represent a sharp departure from the authoritarianism of traditional managerial control. There are a number of incentives for management to respond to this new approach: increased absenteeism and labor turnover; better educated workers challenging the authoritarian atmosphere of the workplace; the struggle to maintain quality production; the realization that the time-worn system of "scientific management" is outmoded and unresponsive to changing cultural attitudes in American society as a whole. The tensions in labor-management relations, however, will not suddenly relax; tough, militant bargaining over issues of a controversial nature will continue. But current trends indicate that unions and management will be jointly developing processes that shift more and more control over the workplace to the hands of the workers and their union representatives.

Involvement of the workers in decision-making related to "managing the enterprise" lies farther down the road. It is an issue of hard controversy, for top management recoils even at the thought of worker representation on boards of directors. The first breakthrough in the United States, widely publicized, came in the 1979 negotiations between the UAW and Chrysler Corporation. It arose out of the dire financial straits in which the corporation found itself, although the issue had already been raised as a UAW demand in its 1976 negotiations with Chrysler. The president of the UAW, pursuant to the negotiated understanding, was elected to the Chrysler board of directors. While the corporation asserted that Fraser's election to the board was made in recognition of his personal attributes and capabilities, Fraser has stated very clearly that he will act as a representative of the workers:

> Q. Just how do you view your role as a member of that board, assuming you're elected next May?

A. In only one way—as a workers' representative. I intend to speak out on behalf of the 125,000 UAW members at Chrysler. I'm going to fight like hell to see that the decisions that Chrysler Corporation makes wind up helping, rather than hurting, the workers. For the first time in the history of our country, workers are going to have a voice at the highest policy-making level of the company.

Q. Won't you have a conflict of interest on the Chrysler board at times?

A. Whenever there is a legitimate problem, obviously I will not participate. I'll leave the room. If the board were to discuss collective bargaining, for example, I would not want to be involved because my clear responsibility, my total responsibility, is to the UAW members.

But on many important questions, there would be no conflict. If Chrysler was considering expanding its overseas operations as it did a few years ago, for example, I'd know about that and be able to argue the issue. In that case, its decision not only cost workers' jobs, it generally proved to be a financial disaster that harmed the company.

Q. Putting a union representative on a corporate board is a major departure from American labor's traditions. What's the rationale behind the tradition?

A. The way things work now, the company does something and the workers react through their union. The company makes the decisions and the workers have to try to alter them once they're made if we don't agree.

Looking down the road, it seems to me, workers are going to have to be a part of the decision-making process. Why should corporations have a sole monopoly on decisions that affect so many workers, their families, and their communities? We must have a voice in our own destiny.[1]

The UAW believes that Fraser will not only have access to information otherwise denied but will be in a position to act as a spokesman in behalf of the workers' interests as issues of special interest arise. Both management and labor will be viewing this breakthrough closely and watching to see whether and where it spreads further.

In fact, Fraser made his presence felt as a representative of the workers within a period of weeks. It was on his initiative that the board formally adopted a resolution dealing with the pressing problem of plant closings and consolidations. The board agreed to establish a Plant Utilization and Human Resources committee to

> ensure that this Corporation consider the human and social factors associated with plant closings and consolidations, and to recommend courses of action which may be followed by this Corporation in connection with such events for the purpose of finding alternative employment for laid-off employes, locating other manufacturing companies which might purchase deactivated facilities, and soliciting government assistance for conversion of such facilities to new technology for the Corporation's or other use.[2]

At least one other large corporation—American Motors—has accepted the union proposal for representation on the board of directors. The government, however, has indicated that the understanding between the parties as currently constituted would run afoul of the law. The issue has not yet been resolved.

A third form of worker involvement in decision-making involves outright worker control of the enterprise. By and large, companies controlled and operated by the workers had been privately owned in the past and had fallen on hard times. To preserve their jobs the workers bought out the owners and took control. The companies involved are comparatively small. Some have failed, others have succeeded brilliantly. A recent example is the Rath Packing Company in Waterloo, Iowa, which was facing bankruptcy. With the approval of the board of directors and by majority vote of the stockholders, the workers will purchase a large block of common stock through an Employee Stock Wage Payment Plan. Although this stock will not represent virtual control by the workers, it is a form of participation which could lead to eventual worker control.

In the past the labor federation of the United States has not looked with favor upon employee participation in decision-making programs. More recently it has called for joint labor-management effort. Individual unions, meanwhile, have become involved through adoption of quality of work-life improvement programs, and interest is increasing at a rapid pace. In the past year the Communication Workers of America (CWA) negotiated with AT&T to establish a national committee to generate initiatives for cooperative labor-management activity among Bell system affiliates. Its purposes include "encouraging greater employee participation." Similar national committees are already in place between the UAW and General Motors, Ford and Chrysler. Dozens of other firms and their unions are engaging in worker participation processes. The concept is spreading rapidly. It represents the next great wave of progress for workers in the ongoing drive for dignity, self-fulfillment, and an enlarged measure of control over their lives in the workplace.

Notes

1. *UAW Solidarity*, 19 November 1979, pp. 7–8.
2. Ibid.

PART IV

The Eurosocialists Speak

11

Democratizing the Political Process

FRANÇOIS MITTERRAND

François Mitterrand headed the French Socialist party (PS) from 1971 until his election as president of France in 1981. Under his leadership, the PS experienced remarkable theoretical innovation and organizational rejuvenation, replacing the French Communist party as the largest party on the French Left and emerging in 1981 with an absolute majority in the national assembly.

Mitterrand eloquently describes the integral place of political democracy in democratic socialist theory and practice. He notes the absence or erosion of basic political rights throughout the world, and calls on democratic socialists both to ensure those rights and to conquer what he calls "new realms of freedom" in this age of complex—and potentially enslaving—technology. According to Mitterrand, both the traditional and the newer freedoms will be secured only by a more democratic, a more participatory, a more responsible citizenry.

DEMOCRATIZING THE POLITICAL PROCESS

François Mitterrand

My subject is political democracy. Of course, for a socialist, democracy means not only political democracy, but economic and social democracy—and, I would add, cultural democracy as well. But without political democracy there can be no socialism. There are capitalist regimes in which no real economic and social democracy exists. Here it is useless to speak of socialism. But there are other countries which are spoken of as socialist, but where there is no freedom. We cannot call this socialism either.

It is a sobering exercise merely to count the number of countries on earth where the rule of law has been reduced to the level of the machine gun, the hangman's rope, exile, prison. And note that many of these countries have guarantees of freedom and human rights written into their constitutions. There are many countries dominated by a capitalist power which really is based on an alliance of oligarchies with dictatorial authority. There are the communist countries whose working class, as in Poland, must fight for basic trade union rights. There are all the Third World countries where underdevelopment has led to the single-party system, to the macroeconomic plan, to bureaucratic structures, and ultimately to widespread poverty despite the wealth of those in power. There are all those countries which are imperialist or expansionist—how else can we understand wars such as that in Vietnam, waged for twenty years by France and then by the United States, followed by a war in Cambodia and now by one in Afghanistan? As for political imperialism, tied as it is to economic and financial oligarchies, how can we fail to see the constant violence that reigns throughout Latin America, especially in Central America? Or the terrorism that has entered into relations between peoples and states? Consider the case of Iran, which seized fifty Americans, undoubtedly in response to the countless acts of terror perpetrated by the former regime which was supported by the Western powers. Then there are the cases of majorities dominating minorities—political, ethnic or religious—and eradicating them. Or the genocidal destruction of an entire people. Yesterday Cambodia, today Timor. The list goes on.

All of this brings socialists to the realization that the first task in their struggle is to establish a rule of law, not only between individuals and social groups, but also between nations. What are those fundamental freedoms and rights that must be protected by law? We find many sources of these rights in our civil law. Some of the most important stem from British tradition. These in turn were incorporated into many constitutions of the original American states (one of the earliest being Massachusetts). The founders of democracy in France eloquently expressed these same rights when they drew up their constitution and the Declaration of the Rights of Man. These fundamental freedoms all are based on one simple principle: popular sovereignty. This means the freedom to come and go as one chooses, the freedom to write, speak, communicate. It means freedom of assembly and association. It means pluralism of opinion within one system. And finally, it means the right of a people to express itself through universal suffrage.

Political democracy came about through a liberal revolution. It was the liberal bourgeoisie which put an end to ancestral feudalism. But by an irony of history, the bourgeoisie, in wielding the powers of production in emerging industrial societies, quickly forgot its principles and began itself to exercise dictatorial powers. So a second revolution was needed. This revolution would be led by socialists—whatever their school of thought—for the purpose of securing *collective* rights and freedoms. These included the right to a job, a salary, security, education, training, culture, housing, rest, leisure. But of course at this point we are discussing social, not political democracy.

Let us return to our subject, and ask ourselves this: what has become of those basic, political freedoms in countries such as ours? Often we find that they are gutted, eroded by time or by private interests. What has become of the right to come and go freely when the powers of the police have been greatly extended? What has become of freedom of expression when modern communications technology is generally in the hands of governments or large corporations? What is the relationship between the police and justice? A democracy gives the last word to its judges—not the first and last word to the police. And yet democracy cannot function without law and order. Obviously it cannot give way to emotion, violence, terrorism. These issues need all of our attention.

There is another area in which our historic freedoms have not been fulfilled. To this day no democracy extends its rights and liberties equally to all its citizens. In many countries it took a long time before women were even granted the right to vote. We still have not clearly defined women's inheritance rights, nor their rights in the area of work. When we talk about unemployment, we usually fail to count women who have never worked or who cannot work. In my country, and I assume in others, women are trained for jobs they end up never doing, or else they work at jobs for which they were never trained. They still earn less pay for equal work. Finally, consider how many countries there are where women have yet to win their rights in personal and family life—I'm thinking in particular of birth control. Like women, children are often castoffs in our societies. If we compare legislation in the countries of the industrial West, we see some disturbing shortcomings. What kind of equal opportunities do children have when education in most democracies is determined by social class?

Yet another category of castoffs is minority groups within societies; this includes groups based on ethnicity, race, skin color, religion. Can we really say that these millions of men and women within our self-proclaimed democracies are truly free? In France, there are hundreds of thousands of immigrants who do not have the same rights as other workers (I believe this to be the case in the

United States as well). And there are many others—factory workers, employees and farmers who have been reduced to poverty, the handicapped—it is easy to overlook the many minority and oppressed social classes that exist in political democracies.

It is the responsibility of socialists both to halt the erosion of our fundamental freedoms and extend them to these very categories of people who have been denied these last two centuries. But we must also conquer what I call "new realms of freedom." Permit me to cite several examples. Many European countries—and many countries elsewhere—suffer from too great a centralization of state power. We will have conquered a new realm of freedom when people have been accorded decision-making powers where they work and where they live. In the United States, of course, there is a real decentralization between the individual states and the federal government. But wouldn't an even more decentralized decision-making process enormously extend fundamental freedoms even in the United States?

Perhaps nowhere is more to be gained than in employer-employee relations. New realms of freedom will be created when workers are called upon to determine, or at least to control, those actions which determine their worklife. New realms of freedom will be created once it is recognized that the entire process of investment in capitalist countries is controlled by private corporations that are increasingly multinational in character. Workers, the working class, everyone who participates in the productive process, must be able to control and determine major investment priorities. New realms of freedom will be conquered once we have expanded the powers of the public sector to compete with the private sector, monopolized as it is by special interests. To whom, after all, do the air, water, underground resources, and major media belong, and by what right can they be appropriated by a person, a family, or a conglomeration?

There is an obvious freedom to conquer—or regain—as we face our role in the destruction of nature. The development of industrialized societies, whether in capitalist or communist countries, took place without regard for the balance of nature. For the first time in human history, mankind has reversed the relationship between himself and nature. Drunk with power, man acts thoughtlessly and destructively. And in destroying, he destroys himself, because he is also a part of nature. If an economic system is based solely on profit, then destruction becomes profitable, because what is destroyed must then be rebuilt, only to be destroyed again in order to be rebuilt—and on and on, with all natural equilibrium fast disappearing. Our oxygen, forests, rivers and oceans cannot be the sole property of a world-wide oligarchy.

And could we not apply the same reasoning as we move away from nature proper and examine the physical and social organization of our towns and cities? Our society seems to suffer from the inability of people to communicate with each other. Ironically, people find themselves alone in the crowd, and so must refind their natural equilibrium.

Socialists have solutions to offer—decentralization of decision-making, protection of our natural environment, the right of people to govern themselves at home and at work and, finally, control over science and technology. Let me elaborate on this last point. Man created the machine, but only revolutionized its use at the beginning of the nineteenth century. The machine came to replace human muscle, leading philosophers to believe that man had released a great liberating force. He had succeeded in creating an extension of himself, and now could devote his time and energy to other things besides exhausting physical labor. But given the economic system of the time, the opposite happened. The machine became an additional means to accelerate production (growth being the only criteria of the system) and in the end man became subject to his own creation, the machine. The newfound freedom became a new and stronger form of oppression. Recall the images—they have not faded—of workers being crushed in the mines, the textile mills, the iron and steel mills.

Today the problem is very much the same. But now the machine replaces not only man's muscle, but his memory and his judgment. The economic system of the nineteenth century used the machine to crush man, as will the economic systems of the twentieth and twenty-first centuries. Socialists know that the workers have been robbed of their physical strength and soon will be robbed of their intelligence too. Socialists must therefore display sufficient imagination to find ways for man to become once again master of his own creation. There are four areas in particular where man must assert social control. First, nuclear energy, which is a highly centralized process; second, computers, which are being used today as a relay between most technologies;

third, telecommunications, which have vast powers to mold the minds of millions without really safeguarding their fundamental liberties; fourth, biology, where science can alter the basic facts of life and death, especially in the field of genetics. And yet socialists must never fear science or man's creative capacities. It is conservatives who turn their backs on progress. So the true mission of socialists is to create structures that will enable modern man to conquer new realms of freedom in defiance of oppressive technologies.

Let me close with three points. First, socialists must fight for what we call "time to live." Social struggles have already won some of these rights. At the beginning of the capitalist era, people spent all their lives working for someone else's benefit. A man would go to work at the age of six or seven and work until he died. It was not until 1841 in France that legislation put an end to the fourteen-hour day in the mines for children under the age of ten. There was no rest, there were no days off, no holidays, no paid vacations, no pensions. When the retirement age finally was set at sixty-five years, the average worker died at age fifty-five. Socialists have a certain view of life. Life is not an appendage of work—work is a means to live.

My second point concerns power and countervailing power. What is power? It is something within ourselves. We tend to feel that someone else is responsible for our problem, which is often the case—the state, the ruling class, the boss, the neighbors, etc. But the problem really lies within ourselves. I often quote to my French comrades a favorite phrase from Thucydides, the Greek historian. It goes something like this: "Every man always goes to the limit of his power." That is true in public and private life. It is also true in the life of a couple and in parent-child relationships. Sometimes one side dominates, sometimes the other. Democracy recognizes these contradictions. Democracy means setting up institutions that make it possible to balance those contradictions, not deny their existence. Socialists recognize that power is necessary in an organized society. Socialists are not anarchists, refusing all power and structure, but they guard against abusive power by setting up countervailing powers. This was the old theme of the first founders of public law, such as Montesquieu. Other methods supplement this separation of powers, and these include decentralization and self-management.

My last point is that socialists must organize society so as to do away with the following menacing powers. First, the power of fear, whether it stems from the machine gun, the noose, exile, torture, death, or from more subtle methods such as corruption, oppression and ignorance. Second, the power of lies. What better means to misinform could those in power possess than state control of the media? This is the case in many countries which dare to call themselves democratic. In many other states, financial and corporate powers control the information process, making a travesty of the free exchange of ideas. Fortunately, there are writers, thinkers, and journalists in every country who retain a strong sense of freedom and a love of their work. Socialists need these people. Third, the power of money. And here we return to our starting point. What kind of socialist accepts the domination of the strongest simply because he is the richest, or because his power is founded on the exploitation of man by man? This applies to nations as well as to individuals. Socialists therefore must concentrate on defining both civil and international law. When we examine the international institutions that are supposed to render justice and keep the peace, we can only conclude that they have failed. Socialism is about securing liberty under the law. It is, lastly, about gaining this superior freedom which we call responsibility—the capacity of each man and woman to take part in the determination of the common good.

(Translated by Nancy Lieber)

12

Democratizing the Social Structure

JOOP DEN UYL

Joop Den Uyl, prime minister of the Netherlands from 1973 to 1977, is the leader of the Dutch Labor party and president of the Confederation of Socialist Parties of the European Community.

His topic is social democracy, or the establishment of greater equality and social justice among people. He describes the vehicle by which most postwar Western European societies achieved this end—the welfare state. Through steeply progressive taxation, revenues were raised to pay for an elaborate system of social welfare programs and services available to all, including health, transportation, education, old-age pensions, even leisure and cultural facilities. This redistribution of income through the public sector helped correct earlier social and financial inequities. Yet the welfare state came under criticism in the 1970s—from the Left for its inadequacies (reformed capitalism was not the same as socialism), and from the Right for its difficulties in a period of limited or no economic growth. Den Uyl candidly outlines the difficulties posed by the international economic system of the 1970s and 1980s, but concludes that the answer is to deepen the role of public powers, to further democratize the social structure and never to retreat from the important gains in equality that have been secured through the welfare state.

DEMOCRATIZING THE SOCIAL STRUCTURE

Joop Den Uyl

Social democrats who visit the United States often have the feeling that they come to preach the social gospel to a paganist, unwilling and resistant people. That is particularly true in these days of the Reagan administration, when the gospel seems to be the defense of nineteenth century establishment values.

Yet the observant visitor soon learns that there is another America, an America that does not accept the inequalities and the shortsightedness of an unjust society, an America that seeks answers to the problems before us all. We social democrats in Europe need this other America in the defense of the welfare state and the democratization of the social structure.

During my term as prime minister, we initiated a scheme for workers to share the ownership of capital. Our bill was never passed by parliament. And why not? One of the major arguments of the Right was that the introduction of such a scheme would frighten American investors and, in fact, some American firms threatened to withdraw their investments from Holland.

So we in Europe need a firm and strong position of the democratic Left in this country. It is not only good for the United States, but for Europe as well. For it cannot be denied that the European welfare state is under attack, and not only in the

207

Britain of Margaret Thatcher—Milton Friedmans are among us all. The growing attacks on the welfare state, of course, have much to do with the world economic crisis afflicting Western European economies. The welfare state has been the creation of a period with rapid economic growth. The decline of economic growth during the seventies poses new questions that must be answered by all socialists who are also political realists.

Social democracy is a force to be reckoned with in Europe. It is the largest political group in the European parliament, a leading power in Germany, Austria, and Scandinavia. And yet, social democracy in Europe is in a difficult position today. It is now the opposition party in Sweden, England, the Netherlands, Ireland, and Portugal.

The following questions are being hotly debated in Europe: Will the welfare state survive the economic crisis now confronting the world? Is democratic socialism dynamic enough to excite a young generation in the postindustrial society? Is democratic socialism capable of solving the economic stagnation in Western society?

European democratic socialism since World War II falls into three distinct periods. The first is the creation and expansion of the social welfare state between 1955 and 1965; the second comprises internal criticism of the welfare state between 1965 and 1975; and the third is the external crisis of the welfare state as a result of the continuing world economic crisis since the mid-seventies.

The Creation and Growth of the Welfare State

After 1945 the creation of a welfare state was the primary goal in practically all the countries of Europe. The war had been fought to overcome Hitler, but equally to put an end to the mass unemployment and the impoverishment which millions had suffered in the thirties under the capitalist system.

The creation of the welfare state meant that the government accepted direct responsibility for maintaining full employment. Central planning institutes were set up for the purpose. Forms of more or less indicative planning emerged in most European countries.

Although the trade unions retained their freedom, the government acquired its own clear responsibility in the formation of wages. The point of departure varied considerably. In Germany, the freedom of employers and employees to negotiate was laid down in the constitution. But within the structure of the "social market economy," there was obvious scope for the government to influence wage formation directly or indirectly. In the Netherlands, a so-called planned wage policy was accepted and carried out up to the early sixties.

Government introduced a system of social insurance under which everybody was insured in principle and entitled to a payment for all eventualities: illness, accident, unemployment, disablement, old age or the death of the breadwinner, and by degrees that payment became indexed to rises in prices.

In addition, government accepted much wider responsibilities in the field of education, health, and welfare than it had done in the past. More and more children between the ages of twelve and eighteen attended school. Health care was nationalized in Britain, where the National Health Service came to be regarded as a major institution of the welfare state. The Netherlands introduced compulsory health insurance based on level of income, with approximately 80 percent of the population qualifying for coverage. The quality of the health system improved radically and health care came to account for a higher percentage of the national income with every passing year.

Welfare also expanded greatly, with many of its new programs designed for specific groups, such as ethnic minorities, young people, the aged, and war victims. Beginning with the idea that the community is responsible for the development of its citizens after they leave school, vast governmental structures were assembled both to educate the general public and provide it with social services. During the mid-fifties in Holland, for example, this trend led to the creation of the Ministry of Cultural Affairs, Recreation and Social Welfare Work. No department's expenditure in the postwar period has risen as sharply as this one.

Democratic socialism has without doubt been of decisive importance in shaping the welfare state. Socialist philosophy and influence is reflected first and foremost in the further emancipation of the working classes. It is also reflected in the growth towards equality, which is the product of the social security system and of the education, health, and welfare facilities. These social changes stem in large part from the plans and designs for society formulated between the two world wars by the Fabians in England, Hendrik de Man in Belgium, and Karl Mannheim.

The building of the welfare state has led to a general feeling of security, an improvement in the standard of living and a reduction in the disparities between incomes, to greater equality and an improvement in the quality of life. In Holland, for example, the welfare state has led to the establishment of a guaranteed social minimum for workers and people dependent on social allowances. Of course, there is still bad housing, pollution, class differences—there are many shortcomings. But what has been achieved is worthwhile defending and never, no matter what the criticisms, will we accept a recurrence of the differences, the exploitation, the discrimination of the capitalist system that we knew. *There is no turning back on the welfare state.*

The fifties, however, concluded with a distinct loss of social momentum. European socialism reconciled itself to a mixed economic order. Many socialist ideals appeared to have been achieved. The trade union movement and democratic socialism became integrated into a social order of a mixed character. But of course socialism is more than the safety and security of the welfare state. Socialism means a new economic order based on a fundamental democratization of society. It means the participation in any sector of those who are dependent on the outcome of the social process. And there is much truth in the criticism that the welfare state meant an improvement of living standards and social security, but that it left the power structure of society unchanged.

During the sixties, socialism began to lose its appeal for the younger generation in many countries. The revolt of the sixties was a movement that was anti-establishment, anti-institutions, and anti-history. In Europe, it was first and foremost a movement directed against a form of democracy perceived as outdated and against a welfare state suffering from ossification. It coincided with opposition to the democracy of bureaucrats, to the numerous new institutions regulating the affairs of the community and attending to its needs *without any real participation whatsoever on the part of the people for whom the arrangements were being made.*

It meant militant refusal to accept the unequal distribution of economic power, and hence opposition to the establishment in all its forms. It meant protest against multinational corporations (and the state bureaucracies that collaborated with them), against the autonomous banking system and the financial centers, against the great inequalities that have always existed in the distribution of property and wealth.

All European socialist parties have experienced the effects of this revolt, albeit they have assimilated the experience in different ways. It led to a rejuvenation of the Dutch Labor party, among both leadership and members, and to a more radical program as well.

The demand for social reform dominated the stance of the socialist parties in the second half of the sixties. Reform was proposed for penal law, for land policy—a major feature being the possibility of compulsory purchase of land by the government for urban redevelopment and physical planning. There were attempts to democratize the governing bodies of universities, schools and social institutions, as well as persistent efforts to give workers the same say in the running of companies as the representatives of capital or the management appointed by capital. There were also attempts to give workers entrepreneurial equity, such as the Meidner Plan in Sweden, and the capital growth distribution project for workers in the Netherlands. The period saw a variety of efforts to take the running of education, health care, and welfare organizations out of the hands of trustees or philanthropic society ladies, and give control to the clients and staff. In schools this involved a transfer of power from administration and traditional school boards to parents, teachers and pupils. In brief, there was an enormous effort to achieve fundamental democracy throughout all the institutions of society.

The years between 1965 and 1975 also witnessed the advent of citizen action groups, which functioned in part as a supplement to parliamentary democratic processes. In this period, democratic socialism generally proved itself to be a stalwart defender of parliamentary democracy, but at the same time it forged successful links with action groups; these gradually became more institutionalized.

Reform is not merely an internal issue. One cannot build up equality in ones own country without taking into account inequal-

ity in the outside world. And so the sights of the socialist parties
were raised beyond national frontiers. There was great sympathy
with Willy Brandt's "Ost-Politik," and vigorous support for the
liberation movements in Latin America and Asia. Indeed, the
shock of the Vietnam War did more to shape the ideas and
thinking in my own party during that period than any other
world political event. Up to the early sixties, the Dutch Labor
Party was one of the most faithful defenders of NATO. Since the
mid-sixties, our membership has been accompanied by rising
criticism. These years also saw the birth of numerous action
groups working for increased development aid and support of
the Third World.

During the first progressive cabinet in the Netherlands with a
socialist majority, which I led between 1973 and 1977, the government raised development aid to 1½ percent of the net national income. In fact, the Third World movement functioned as
a new ideological dimension of the welfare state. In my country it
has become perhaps the major pillar of the ideology of democratic socialism, the new vehicle of the idea of equality. One might
say that there are three pillars underpinning this new ideology.
The first is that of a further development towards equality of
participation and income through the democratization of the
power structure. The second is solidarity with the Third World,
and the third is opposition to an unlimited spread of nuclear
energy and above all to the nuclear arms race. It is expressed in
the political willingness on the part of the Netherlands to take
unilateral steps to limit the nuclear tasks it fulfills within NATO.

In the decade from 1965 to 1975, it was not only the left wing
that railed against the welfare state, but the right as well. A
regrouping of reactionary forces began to take shape in the early
seventies. In America, it found its most readily identifiable center
in Milton Friedman's Chicago school of welfare economics.
Friedman's *Capitalism and Freedom* (1968) helped initiate a right-
wing revival in Europe that made a considerable impact. The
revival focused on the recovery of competitive capitalism, the
restoration of free enterprise operating in a free market, and
cutbacks in the public sector. Friedman's conclusions—that the
further growth of the public sector is identified with the demise of
political democracy—did not pass unnoticed in Europe. Freedom
is seeking its revenge on equality. The levelling of incomes is

branded as a threat to the privileged and as the first sign of cultural impoverishment.

These are all themes which can be found in various forms in the development of the New Right in America. They first appeared in the majority of European countries in the course of the seventies, and have undoubtedly played a role in the losses experienced by many socialist parties in elections during the last several years.

However, before examining how socialist parties should respond to this attack upon the welfare state, let us devote some attention to the current trials the welfare state is undergoing as a result of the crisis in the world economy.

The Challenge of the International Economic Crisis

Heralded by the energy crisis in the autumn of 1973, an international economic crisis arrived in 1974; its structural character was only belatedly recognized by the socialists and other parties. In general, the European socialist parties adhered to the official analysis of the crisis, as set forth in the report of the McCracken Committee set up by the OECD (Organization for Economic Cooperation and Development) in the spring of 1977. Economic recession, according to the writers of the report, was a product of an annoying concurrence of chance events: inflation, the devaluation of the dollar, the rise in oil prices, and over-capacity in certain sectors. But there was absolutely no reason whatsoever for assuming that the world economy would not resume the normal growth rhythm of the fifties and sixties. Fortunately, two-and-a-half years later a new OECD study entitled *Interfutures* displayed a considerably greater understanding of the structural nature of the slowdown in growth and the changed relations in the world economy.

The rise of new industrial centers in the Third World countries would exercise a lasting constraint on the Western economy's capacity for growth. The rise in oil prices and other raw materials was an expression both of the fundamental and continuing scarcity and of the newly won power of the oil-producing countries. Protection of the environment would mean that the cost of industrial production would increase and growth would be permanently inhibited.

There has also been a shift in values: people in the postindustrial society are more interested in the quality of their work and in having more leisure time than in the level of their income. *Interfutures* describes this attitude as "postmaterialist."

Although the United States, geographically speaking, has enormously greater potential for expansion than Europe, most Western economies will be forced to reckon with a low annual growth of perhaps 2–2½ percent. That has enormous consequences for the future of the welfare state. In the first place, we must choose for or against the concept of a society in which a few people work and earn a lot of money, while many are excluded from working life. I reject this model, because in fact it would mean legitimizing terrible inequalities. Socialism must choose for a society in which nobody who wants to work is deprived of the opportunity to do so. This means that jobs have to be created in services, in the non-market sector, and that there has to be large-scale redistribution of the available work among more people. The serious consequences of this are a reduction in the income of those employed and a greater emphasis on the total income and purchasing power of the social unit.

There are other consequences. In a period during which capitalism has lost its driving force of uninhibited expansion, it is more crucial than ever that levels of employment not be left to the whims of the market. If the economic process is not ordered and controlled in a situation of low growth, we have the prospect of mass unemployment (one of the factors responsible being the inevitable march of technological progress).

Socialist parties and governments have generally responded to the crisis with the tried and tested instruments of the Keynesian school. They have raised government spending and have been out to maintain the purchasing power of the workers. Up to a certain point this policy is the right one, but it is not the right solution for every problem. In fact, by attempting to maintain and increase real wages, the European trade unions may be barring the way to a recovery in employment. The European Trade Union Confederation (ETUC) has been pursuing a different tack for some time now. A redistribution of the available work is the current focus of its efforts, not wage increases. For one thing, by reducing the workweek, women will be given greater work opportunities. In the Netherlands, 20 percent of women belong to the work force. They are still discriminated against, but women must be given the same chance as men to work (I wish to be quite clear: feminism is an integral part of socialism. And it means that men too must reconsider their role in society—in the factory, in the household, in the raising of children).

The idea that unemployment can be combatted by major boosts to purchasing power is by no means dead. But under these changed circumstances, there is only one boost to purchasing power that can be justified according to democratic socialist principles. That is a greater transfer of income and capital from the richest countries to the poorest countries in the Third World. Here is the uncompromising message of socialism in the eighties. I am in favor of steering capital flows, investments and incomes by a democratically controlled government. I am aware that a policy of this kind can only succeed if it is based on the workers having a real say about capital flows and investments at the level of individual companies and branches of industry. I am also aware that a policy of this kind can only be put into effect if there is more widespread recognition of the nature of the new relations in the world economy and of the need for a new approach in Europe and the United States.

As chairman of the Confederation of Socialist Parties of the European Community, I have made some suggestions in the past year and have taken some initiatives which I would like to repeat here. The first relates to the cutthroat competitive battle which is being waged among Japan, the United States and Europe in the development and application of microelectronics. The Japanese are in the lead, America is a good second and Europe is limping in third place.

The application of microelectronics and microprocessors in particular may be of great value in replacing heavy, dirty and monotonous work. Microelectronics can make a major contribution to improving the quality of work, protecting the environment, saving energy and raw materials, and improving communications and information services. But microelectronics may lead (and will, if applied wholesale) to millions of workers being made redundant, because although the increase in productivity may be guaranteed, there is no safeguard that sales will follow a similar trend in the stagnating economy we possess now. If microelectronics are introduced without constraint or consultation as to their effects, they will constitute a huge threat to employment not only in Western society, but also in the Third World.

What course of action should we take? We have precedents. When people realized in the course of the sixties that a deliberate policy was needed to protect the environment, the United Nations convened the World Environmental Conference in Stockholm in 1972. The conference led to some standardization of requirements for industry and transport in order to combat environmental pollution. It has proved a blessing in numerous respects. I think it is high time that, at the initiative of the United Nations and with the ILO (International Labor Office) as the implementary body, we agree on common standards and measures as to how and at what pace new and existing technologies should be applied. We need to gain control of these technologies before they lead us into a new slavery. This task cannot be left to the free market, or we will face mass unemployment.

Consider another initiative. At the instigation of Jan Tinbergen (a dedicated socialist and winner of the Nobel Prize for economics), Wim Kok, chairman of the European Trade Union Confederation, Jan Pronk, assistant secretary-general of UNCTAD, (United Nations Conference on Trade and Development) and I drafted a proposal for a world employment. The essence of it is to set targets for the growth of existing industries in all economic areas in the world. The first attempt at a planned approach of this kind was undertaken in 1969 by the ILO on the occasion of its fiftieth anniversary. The attempt came to naught because of the crisis of the seventies. It is high time that a new plan of this kind, which for now we have called the New World Employment Plan, be drawn up. I discussed it two days ago with Kurt Waldheim. I think it is a necessary complement to the Brandt commission's report. It expresses the conviction that the necessary adjustment of Western industry to the economic development of the Third World is only acceptable and can only be achieved within the framework of targets based on the mutual interest of both the industrialized and the developing countries. We need a new international economic order, or we will face increasing disorder.

The Future of the Welfare State

Democratic socialism is based on belief in the fundamental equality of mankind, and socialists will defend the welfare state that has contributed so much to greater equality. Yet we must realize that the last decade of our century will see an economy with little growth, which requires increased regulation and control; despite this, the public sector must be extended and strengthened. Democratic socialism advocates the solidarity of workers and non-workers, the right of workers and citizens to decide about their work and their living conditions.

The welfare state is under attack. The argument of the Right is that too few people work to supply the income for too many who do not work. The answer is that a free market economy will worsen this process. Full employment is a prerequisite of the welfare state, and planning, sharing of jobs and income are the prerequisites of full employment in the troubled economy of the eighties.

The Right also attacks a high level of government expenditure (except, of course, for defense) but forgets that a high level of government expenditure in the 1970s proved to be the most stabilizing factor in an economy which needs management. In fact, perhaps the most essential difference between the 1930s and now is a comparatively high level of government expenditure that prevents a recurrence of the depression and mass unemployment of that time. Socialists therefore defend the high level of taxation and government expenditure. This is not a popular position, but it is necessary.

The Right also attacks the welfare state for abuses in payments and services. And of course the state has a duty to fight tax evasion and social security abuses. But the real problem is of a different order: is it reasonable even to expect responsible behavior from people in a society predicated on the inequitable distribution of wealth and power? The masses of workers would be powerless if it were not for the unions which defend them.

Socialism is based on equality and equal rights of human beings. We will master the problems ahead only if we proceed to democratize the social structure of our societies with all the conviction we hold.

13

Democratizing the Economy

OLOF PALME

Olof Palme leads the Social Democratic party of Sweden and served as prime minister from 1969 to 1976. He is currently chair of the United Nations Independent Commission on Disarmament and Security Issues, which is patterned after the earlier Brandt commission on North-South issues.

Palme completes the definition of democratic socialism with a discussion of economic democracy. Democratic socialists argue that, contrary to its theorists, the capitalist system of production and distribution is not controlled by the consumers, but by private, corporate power. What is produced and how it is produced is determined by autocratic management, and prices are not set by the free market mechanism but by oligopolies and monopolistic practices. Democratizing the economic system, Palme tells us, means a greater role for government in creating and maintaining full employment, a democratically planned management of the economy, a renewal of working life through increased workers' participation and a democratization of the process of capital formation and investment decisions. He illustrates these steps by drawing on the Swedish experience of the last decade, an experience that probably goes furthest in Western Europe in opening up the economic system to popular control.

DEMOCRATIZING THE ECONOMY

Olof Palme

Democratic socialism is above all a freedom movement. It represents a century-long struggle for democracy and social justice. At the turn of the century, our pioneers fought against a ruthless class society to obtain the right to vote—to obtain political democracy. The next step was to overcome misery and injustice—to obtain social democracy. And now, social democrats from all over the world are discussing the next step of our struggle—economic democracy. Although our methods may differ and our national conditions vary, we are all united in the conviction that there will be no true democracy unless we also obtain democracy in the economic life. It is no coincidence that we are supporting the demands for a new economic world order and at the same time are also demanding a new economic order in our own countries.

Within the international socialist movement there is fundamental agreement much on basic values and concepts. François Mitterrand recently said that each of the socialist parties chooses its own path, but there is no socialism unless all have a clear understanding of what they have in common, which is the relentless struggle against all forms of exploitation of man by man. Thus the problems I will deal with we all have in common. But if I speak a great deal about our experience in Sweden it is to avoid being too abstract, simply to put flesh on the bones of theory. It is the country I know best.

Democracy is the heart of socialism. Democracy links together democratic socialists from various countries, brings together democratic socialists from different generations. For us, democracy is a question of human dignity. This includes the political liberties, the right to freely express our views, the right to criticize and to influence opinion. It embraces the right to health and work, to education and social security. It is closely connected with the right and the actual opportunity to work with others in shaping the future together. These democratic rights cannot be reserved for a certain class of society. They must belong to all the people.

In Sweden, as in many other countries, the struggle for political democracy was carried out by social democrats with the aid of the bourgeois Left. But when this struggle was won, their ways parted. To the working masses who assembled for the great suffrage demonstrations at the beginning of the century, democracy offered the hope of rising out of misery and poverty. The first demonstrators carried two banners: "Universal suffrage" and "8 hour working day." The two goals were connected; only through democracy could the eight hour working day be realized. But the bourgeoisie was united in its resistance to state intervention, and it tried to convince people that there was a limit to political democracy, that it could not be used to change social conditions. The Social Democratic party, on the other hand, always regarded political democracy as a way to achieve social progress. One of the most prominent figures in the history of the Swedish Social Democratic party, Ernst Wigforss, had consistently maintained that "once you have openly approved the democratic principle of equality, you cannot arbitrarily limit its application to certain areas of life."[1]

Ernst Wigforss's ideas are not dated, as is apparent in this passage from the early seventies on democracy in industrial firms by the Swedish Confederation of Trade Unions: "For the individual, life is of one piece. There is no sharp line between work, economy, culture, social status and treatment. Seen from the individual's perspective, the struggle for liberation and equality must be carried on unceasingly within all sectors of social life."[2] The starting-point of our demand for economic democracy is thus the conception of democracy as a desirable value in itself. As our party program expresses it:

> To the Social Democratic Party, the demand for economic democracy is as self-evident as the demand for political democracy. Social democracy is opposed to an order of things which entitles owners of private capital to wield power over people. It is opposed to every concentration of economic power in the hands of the few. It seeks to place the direction of production and the distribution of the results of production under democratic control. The aim is to make all members of society equal partners in the task of administering and increasing productive resources."[3]

Another starting-point is the fundamental difference between the capitalist and the socialist view of work. It often seems that consumption is the lone social goal of capitalism. Work is a necessary evil, a means of buying the essential qualities of life. It is in freedom from work that people are supposed to gain community, self-realization and a meaningful life. Marx had already pointed to the fact that Adam Smith saw work as a curse.

Socialists, on the other hand, uphold the value of work in modern industrial society. As expressed in our party program,

> Social Democracy maintains that work is the foundation of all well-being and that the willingness of the people to work is the nations' most important asset. Each individual is entitled to participate in working life according to his or her capacity. Each individual is entitled to work which can be experienced as meaningful. Work must form part of a social context in which the fruits of labor are used for the satisfaction of individual and common needs. For this reason the right of determination over production must be vested in the entire nation. Production must be organized in such a way that each individual is esteemed and respected for the work he or she does. It must be organized in such a way that each individual can feel that his or her life and health are safe at work. Employees must therefore be enabled to influence conditions in the firms where they work."[4]

Here again there is an interplay between democracy as a desirable end in itself and as a means to achieve reform.

Thus economic democracy or "democratizing the economy" contains a variety of issues. I will discuss several of these, including the scope of government or state intervention in the functioning of the economy, the renewal of working life, participation of workers in management and the democratization of capital formation.

Let us begin with state intervention in the economy and full employment. The ideas of John Maynard Keynes in the thirties were of tremendous importance. Keynes was an economist in the liberal tradition whose work stimulated a revolution in liberal, macro-economic theory. But the implications were more far-reaching. His theories also had a profound effect on political thinking. What the socialists had arrived at from an ideological standpoint—that the state could and should control the workings of the economy and fight unemployment—was affirmed by modern economic theory. Keynes proved that such action could be taken within the framework of a market economy, which made his position also acceptable to advocates of unfettered free-enterprise.

For years the Keynesian message—the justification of political measures to stabilize the economy and achieve full employment—was the established wisdom in economic policy as well as in economic theory. But in recent years things have changed. Milton Friedman and other laissez-faire economists claim that political measures to stabilize the economy only make things worse. Government should do one job only: fight inflation by controlling the growth of money supply. Public services should be limited to a minimum. The "invisible hand" of the market will accomplish all the rest. The severe crisis in the international economy, with ever-increasing unemployment and with inflation and taxation hollowing out real income, provides a fertile breeding ground in society for these "new liberal" thoughts, always most ardently preached by conservatives. The political message, as we are all very much aware, is that government action and public services limit the freedom of the individual. This message is totally unacceptable to socialists.

I found it most refreshing to read what John Kenneth Galbraith said at Berkeley earlier this year: "Let us see this attack on community for what it is—an attack on our sense of compassion, a revolt against the poor, a design for alienating the least fortunate, an assault on the greatest sources of our pride."[5] I would like to join in his plea that we should all be evangelists for a revived sense of community against the new cult of self.

These arguments provide quite sufficient grounds for renouncing the ideas of Friedman and others. But there are even stronger arguments. For the last year and a half Great Britain has been subject to a full-scale monetarist experiment, which should answer the very pertinent question: Does monetarism work? A week ago *Business Week* gave the following description of what has happened:

> When the Thatcher government took over, in April 1979, the inflation rate was 10.1%, wage settlements averaged 15%, the economy was stagnating, and unemployment stood at 5.5%. Today, inflation is up to 15%, wages are increasing at about 26%, the economy is in free-fall, and the unemployment rate has already moved beyond Depression levels, to 8.5%. Conditions are so bad that many businessmen wonder what will be left of Britain's industrial base when the Thatcher experiment has run its course.[6]

It seems to me that governments all over the world should think more than once before joining the monetarist experiment.

Democratic socialists have always believed that the predominant objective for economic policy must be to achieve and maintain full employment. No problems can be solved by dissolving social security or cutting down heavily in public services. Quite apart from the effects such policies have on the distribution of welfare, they reduce total demand and thus economic growth. Under-utilization of a nation's productive resources is always irrational. Measures that promote social and economic equality also promote social stability which in turn is a prerequisite for re-creating balanced economic growth without inflation.

Full employment is the basis of freedom. The unemployed have little freedom. Few things are more degrading to a human being than to be told: you are not needed, you have no useful role to play in society. For the individual it is a very important part of economic democracy to be able to choose his job freely, to change his job, to receive training when necessary for other employment. The number of unemployed is now approaching 25 million in the advanced industrial OECD countries. Half of them are young people. This is a tremendous threat to individual freedom and to democracy in modern society. To create full employment again requires a tremendous act of liberation from the shackles of an outmoded economic system.

It will happen only if we plan to make it happen. Democratic control of the economy can no longer be confined to traditional methods for stabilizing the economy. Indeed, one of the prerequisites of economic democracy is for civic influence to function on all levels of the economy. The entire field of economic activity must be coordinated by means of *planned management under popular control*. Discussion about planning, unfortunately, tends to be loose and abstract. For this reason we tried to be specific in our party program about those areas in which planning should take place.

First, providing work for all calls for a long-term employment policy aimed at achieving a steady rise in the number of job opportunities. This policy must be combined with measures to eliminate the obstacles preventing many people from participating in working life. The planned management of resources also aims at a fair distribution of the results of production. In order to ensure that there is enough of everything to distribute, planning should also aim at balancing the contents of production so as to provide for the needs of the people. In other words, needs that cannot properly be met by the market economy should be catered to through the public sector.

Planning includes controlling technological development. Technological progress changes the structure of the economy and the conditions of working life. To control our own future, we must control technological development and focus it on the safeguarding and improvement of the living environment and popular health. Accordingly, the evaluation and management of technological progress have become a public task of increasing importance.

We must aim at a responsible management of raw materials and energy. Continued economic growth implies severe strains on raw materials. Through long-term planning we must prevent the exhaustion of these assets. As for energy, planning concerns not only how energy is produced, but how it is used. Saving and economizing are prerequisites for the attainment of reasonable goals.

We must be responsible not only for our use of raw materials and energy, but also for the environment we live in. We must formulate nationwide environmental policy objectives and acquire the means of achieving them. Otherwise we cannot protect nature, preserve our land and water resources, or fight pollution and contamination.

A planned economy must also aim at combating inflation. This includes policies for a fair distribution of incomes in order to reduce compensatory wage claims. It means curbing speculation. And finally, planning must aim at regional balance by evenly distributing employment and services throughout the country. This calls for long-term planning and effective means of supplying assistance to different regions.

To some people of course, the word "planning" has an ugly ring. I should hasten to explain that democratic socialists have no interest whatsoever in creating a gigantic centralized bureaucracy that may easily become cut off from reality and fettered by detailed regulations. We must organize the economy as an open, varied system, not as a fixed, closed one. It should not assume the form of detailed regulations inhibiting the capacity of individuals and firms for initiatives and vigorous economic activity.

Theoretically, it is an advantage to have technocratic planning models; they create—at least on paper—simple solutions to all problems of society. But there are horrifying examples of how this works in practice. In a democracy it is an advantage to build upon countervailing forces which in themselves help to guarantee basic political rights and create ample room for initiative. It is therefore very important to find ways and means of having a broad democratic participation in planning. Planning is no act of mindless machinery. Political decisions are based on value judgments and should not be left to experts or professionals. They can and should be reached by ordinary people.

The planned economy is a step in the democratization of the economy; its corollary—and an important goal of the labor movement in the seventies—is our desire for a renewal of working life. Let me explain what this "renewal" involves with the aid of a Swedish writer, Sven Lindqvist. In his essay, "The Worker Who Began to Wonder," Lindqvist describes a worker who goes to his job every morning past apartment houses, hospitals, schools and theaters. All these buildings look very different from his factory—more attractive, more inviting. He watches an old leather factory in the town being converted into a high school. It is thoroughly remodelled, as if another kind of people would be entering the building. Restaurants are built, auditoriums, rooms for recreation and for various activities. The remodellers make a determined effort to put the individual pupil in the center of things. That was great, he thought. But he began to wonder why they did not build a factory that put the individual worker in the center.

In an encyclopedia he found out that houses, hospitals, theaters and shops are buildings for consumption, meant to satisfy needs. A factory, on the other hand, is a unit of production which exploits human working power and material resources to produce goods or means of production. Goods can be produced in one place, sold in another and used in a third. Goods don't smell, even if the workplace is stinking and noisy. And since the users of the goods never have to set foot in the production site, there is no reason to build more humane factories. Therefore, says Sven Lindqvist's worker, a factory looks like it does and is going to keep on looking that way until my friends and I can get in there and help decide how it is going to look.

Lindqvist's analysis may be incomplete and unfair in certain respects. Still, it helps convey why the labor movement has made such strenuous efforts to renew working life. It might be said that we have broadened the concept of welfare to encompass the conditions of production. We could not be responsible for efforts in health and welfare, while ignoring miserable and dangerous conditions for people involved in production. We could not forge tremendous improvements in the modern infrastructure—better housing, schools, hospitals, roads—while ignoring the place where people produced the goods which laid the foundation for these improvements. We could not purposefully carry out the principles of equal treatment in our social legislation, while silently permitting exceptions for people in certain categories of working life. Nor could we talk about decision-sharing in various areas of public life, without at the same time making an effort to bring about a democratization of the workplace.

The values and goals of a welfare society include security, equality, solidarity, and democracy. But all too often these values are set aside in the business world, where decisions on investments, personnel policy and production methods are largely determined by the profits they will bring to the owners of capital. The free market forces can at times be brutal to individuals, groups, or entire communities. This fundamental social contradiction, strengthened by a number of very thorough reports on the actual working conditions in industry, became the basis for renewed demands for economic democracy in many countries towards the end of the sixties and the early seventies.

The ideology has proved no problem. In economic democracy, workers' right to participate in decision-making is justified by work itself, by the fact that the worker provides the employer with his most valuable asset, his time and his capacity for work. A number of reforms were passed during the first half of the seventies to bring practice into line with theory. The reformers proceeded with care, realizing that changes in legislation and agreements do not in themselves create a workable form of democracy. It is also important that the trade union organizations have the means to perform their new tasks. Otherwise laws and agreements will be reduced to mere formalities with no practical significance. On the other hand, legislation had to reach far enough to provide scope for real change in the work environment.

We found that co-determination proves most effective when as many people as possible participate in the process, and when it deals with problems and concerns close to the employees' own experience and knowledge. Some of the most important provisions include:

- The law on work environment, which covers important points on co-determination in the whole sphere of the work environment. Among other things it enables a union representative to stop production if his working comrades are subject to serious risk of accident. Union representatives also must be informed of all proposed change in plant layout and equipment, and may hold up these changes on grounds of health or safety.
- The law on security of employment, which protects workers against unwarranted dismissal.
- The law on the status of shop stewards, which gives trade union representatives the right to move around at will in

places of work and to receive paid leave when necessary to fulfill trade union obligations.

- The law on representation on the boards of companies, which provides for two worker representatives on the board of directors or governing body of all firms, including government agencies. This means that thousands of blue-and white-collar workers have been able to enter the board rooms, receive information and insight, and represent their colleagues in long-term decisions about the development of the firm.

- The law on co-determination is the most important of the new laws. It gives the trade unions the right to negotiate on all issues concerning work organization and management of the enterprise, and the right to information on all issues within the company.

These reforms have increased employee participation in the decision-making process of companies and other economic organizations. It has granted workers the right to take an active part in forming their work environment, to influence everyday routine in their place of work, but also to have a say in strategic decisions made on the top management level. But we are still in the first years of their implementation, it is still too early to pass final judgment.

A more recent and very controversial issue concerns democratizing capital formation. Employees should have a share in the growth of productive capital. Their participation will help achieve a more equitable distribution of income and wealth, and also increases their influence in the companies where they work and in the economy in general. The Swedish labor movement therefore views sharing in the growth of capital as a complement to labor legislation reform.

Sweden has been discussing wage-earner funds for a number of years. Certain conditions peculiar to our society have strongly influenced this debate. Capital assets in general are unevenly distributed in Sweden, and stock ownership even more so. Stock-owner influence in companies is significantly more concentrated than stock ownership, which means that we have a tremendous concentration of economic power in private business. The allegiance of the trade union movement to the wage policy of solidarity also affects the debate. The principle of equal wages for equal work, regardless of the ability of an individual company to pay wages, favors companies with high productivity. They receive, at least temporarily, an unexploited margin for wage increases in the form of high profits.

The initial work on wage-earner funds was carried out by Rudolf Meidner, economist in the Confederation of Trade Unions. His proposal was based on general profit sharing. The funds should be comprehensive and collective. A central equalization fund was to receive the returns on fund capital. Meidner's plan, published in 1975, stimulated further debate. Thousands of people in the labor movement have studied and discussed the subject. It has met fierce resistance from private industry and bourgeois parties because it affects the rights of private property. It is presently being studied by a government committee that is expected to publish its first report in the near future.

The state of the Swedish economy has changed since 1975. Today the industrial sector of the economy is too small. Total capital formation is insufficient and investment in private industry is particularly insufficient. The solvency of private companies needs improving. At the same time prospects for increases in real wages in the years to come are bleak. This poses, at least in part, a new problem. How are we going to increase capital formation without adding even more to the concentration of private wealth and power? Is a marked increase in company profits (the traditional way to improve solvency and increase private investment) compatible with wage settlements yielding very little or no rise in real wages?

For the Swedish labor movement the answer has been quite simple. The necessary increase in capital formation can be realized only in the form of collective saving. In the short run, employees will have to give up a fraction of their purchasing power in order to increase investments in industry. Employees will not be willing to make that sacrifice, however, if the result is simply increased wealth for capital owners. Nor will they contribute without having an influence over the use of the capital resulting from their sacrifice.

The trade union movement and the Social Democratic party are now in agreement on the goals for wage-earner funds. They are:

- to supplement the wage policy of solidarity;
- to counteract the concentration of wealth;
- to increase wage earners' influence over the economic process; and
- to contribute to collective savings and capital formation for productive investments.

We have not yet decided formally how these funds should be collected and administered, but will have to do so soon. It is clear, however, that the financing of wage-earner funds will have to combine a profit-sharing system with contributions in the form of a percentage of the total wage costs. Funds should be used for long-term investments requiring venture capital, which to a large extent means purchase of stocks. This will naturally have important effects on the economy.

It is useful to remember that self-financing through profits may actually have adverse effects on the economy (quite apart from the concentration of wealth). It is possible to arrive at such a conclusion even by way of the reasoning typical of liberal economic theory. Investment financed largely by profits, after all, does not guarantee an optimal use of capital because the fresh capital is locked up in those companies where the profits were created. This means that the capital is not channeled through the capital market. Consequently, there is no test on what is the most efficient use of capital.

A related point. With high inflation rates businessmen naturally try to protect the value of the capital they are administering. Frequently this means turning to speculation in fixed assets or to financial manipulations. This is a very unproductive use of capital viewed from the perspective of the national economy. Employees, on the other hand, are not interested in speculation. They want good, secure jobs. They are interested in creating new job opportunities. They want to use capital for productive investment. That is also in the interest of the whole nation.

Wage-earner funds will contribute to the functioning of the economy and help us return to a state of balanced economic expansion. They will aid our aims to shape a moral, equal, and just society. They will complement labor legislation in giving workers influence over their own working conditions and on the economy in general.

It must be stressed that the road to economic democracy requires many steps. There is not *one* reform or *one* measure that we can hold out and say: When we have put this into effect, then we have realized economic democracy. We must try many different ways. We must learn from experience.

This last point is important. We do not believe that everything we hope and yearn for can be accomplished overnight. We harbor no illusions that progress will come easy. Ours is a reformist movement. In democratizing the economy we will take one step at a time and work out the next step on the basis of what we have learned. With each step our awareness and knowledge will increase. We know that practice is just as important as theory.

Our methods of change are not for everyone. After the liberation of Portugal in 1974, Rosa Coutinho and Otelo de Carvalho visited Sweden to study democracy in action. They were informed about our new labor laws, and one asked a trade union representative: "How long will it take before these laws are fully in operation?" Their answer: "Some twenty years." They were thunderstruck. For a true revolutionary twenty hours is a long time. Reformism, on the other hand, is a slow process. But it is the only way of really transforming society based on the ideals of democracy.

Notes

1. Tideus Förlag, *Socialism e vår tid* (Stockholm, 1971), p. 19.
2. Swedish Confederation of Trade Unions (LO), Congress, Stockholm, September 1971.
3. *Program of the Swedish Social Democratic Party*, 1975, p. 6.
4. Ibid., pp. 6–7.
5. John Kenneth Galbraith, "Two Pleas at Berkeley," *New York Review of Books* 27, no. 12 (17 July 1980): 25.
6. "Reagan's Top Problem: Braking Inflationary Expectations," *Business Week* 2665 (1 December 1980): 107.

14

A Program for Survival

WILLY BRANDT

Willy Brandt was chancellor of the Federal Republic of Germany
from 1969 to 1974. Currently he is the leader of the German
Social Democratic Party (SPD) and president of the Socialist
International, an organization whose members include some
sixty-five social democratic, democratic socialist, and labor parties
from six continents.

In the last few years, Brandt has turned his attention to
questions of world survival. Despite the high standards of living
achieved in the "First World" (and led by the Western European
social democracies), our very survival, Brandt observes in this
speech, is threatened if we don't resolve three global challenges.
First, the crisis in the world economic order and the social strife
that emerges as economic growth wanes; second, the East-West
arms race and possible nuclear self-destruction; and third,
North-South disparities, beginning with the most basic of natural
resources—food. For Brandt, the answers to these challenges are
obvious: a new international economic order, continued detente
and further arms reduction, and real redistribution of wealth and
resources from the rich to the poor countries. What is missing,
Brandt observes, is the political will on the part of the superpow-

ers to move in these directions. Like the message of Mitterrand, Den Uyl, and Palme, Brandt concludes that the democratic socialist way is one which combines "human inventiveness *and* social responsibility," that the path to survival lies in assuring liberty, equality, and solidarity.

A PROGRAM FOR SURVIVAL

Willy Brandt

"A Program for Survival"—that is the subtitle of the United Nations report published by the Independent Commission on International Development Issues at the beginning of this year. Our intention was to make it clear that North-South tensions represent a dangerous time-bomb—a time-bomb that threatens our very existence. But it is not the only threat to our survival.

I wish to address three decisive challenges now facing the human race, and attempt to outline how we might respond in rational political terms to these challenges in the eighties. In my view, such response would make it more probable that mankind will survive. At the same time, I would like to add the following observation—it reflects my firm belief: Without a substantial contribution by the forces of democratic socialism in many parts of the world, these responses will never be translated into reality.

Anyone who turns his attention to this first year of the 1980s will surely agree: we are experiencing a dramatic development on a world-wide scale. It is not a process of easily measurable change, but a series of wide-ranging upheavals in science and thinking, in economic affairs and in international relations. The numerous crises precipitated in many parts of the world provide ample evidence of this radical change. Yet it would be quite pointless to

237

allow ourselves to be hypnotized by that suggestive word "crisis." There is no hope of things simply righting themselves and returning to "normalcy."

This world-wide change is marked by three dominant factors: the profound restructuring of the world's economy; the persistent East-West rivalry and concomitant arms build-up; and the completely unsatisfactory relations between the Northern industrialized states on the one hand and the developing nations on the other.

Let us consider the first factor, the profound change in the pattern of the world's economy. The period of persistent economic growth in our Western industrial societies seems to be over for the forseeable future. The difficulties we face are characterized by inflation and unemployment, by expensive energy and raw materials and lavish environmental control measures, by high balance-of-payments deficits and an international currency system which has come apart at the seams.

We do not need to look far for the social and political consequences. For a long time it was possible in countries like ours to offset social tensions because there was enough economic growth to go round for all, or almost all. As a result, even the broad masses in our nations enjoyed a steadily rising level of affluence. Whenever divergent interests met head-on, a material compromise was at hand. Today, this handy instrument is available on a limited scale only. In the United Kingdom as in France, in the Federal Republic of Germany as in the United States, the pace of social strife has quickened.

It will require a wide measure of imagination and sensitivity to do justice to the various groups and classes in our modern industrial societies, and at the same time to maintain a smoothly functioning state. If this balance between the various interests is not achieved, there will be an acceleration of a trend already noticeable: a loss of confidence in the competence of those in political office and a dwindling faith in the viability of democracy. The consequence would be a growing alienation which already prevails among certain sections of the young generation—an escapism (as perceived by those of us who believe our societies well worth salvaging) inspired by a blend of political weariness and anxiety about modern civilization.

Those who profit from this alienation would be such groups and philosophies which reject both the present and the future it is likely to usher in. Misgivings about the whole purpose of technical progress might combine with a dangerous nostalgia for the apparent peacefulness and tranquility of former times—a peacefulness and tranquility which never really existed.

And now to the second factor likely to determine the fate of us all in the 1980s—the whole nexus of relations between East and West and the concomitant and persistent arms race.

Our new decade did not make a very promising start. The precarious relationship between the superpowers, marked for years by ups and downs, has once more deteriorated appreciably. The arms race has not only continued apace, but also assumed dimensions which can no longer by grasped by the human mind. The sum of money spent on armaments this year will be 500 billion dollars. Let me repeat this figure: 500,000 million dollars. The industrial states in East and West alone spend 365 dollars per capita on armaments—a sum well about the annual average income in many developing countries. And the developing countries themselves, taken as a whole, spend more on arms than on education and health care for their people. Every warning of the dangerous consequences seems to fall on deaf ears. All the efforts to limit arms levels seem to be frustrated by the feeling of a growing threat from the other side. Sometimes they miscarry because the overall situation becomes too unstable.

We have just seen another example of this instability. The second treaty on the limitation of strategic offensive arms (SALT II), the subject of slow-moving negotiations over a period of many years, has not been ratified. All that remains is the hope of a return to this issue in some other way.

Let us take another illustration. In the mid-seventies the danger loomed of a fresh arms race involving medium-range missiles in Europe, the so-called theater nuclear weapons. Yet only now, this autumn, when it was almost too late, has a start been made on negotiations. It is small wonder then that many people are beginning to ask whether the policy of detente has failed and what alternative there might be. My answer to that is as follows: it may be that the policy of detente—regardless how we define the content of that formula—will not survive the 1980s.

But the only probable alternative would be some form of catastrophe.

No-one should fool himself that we can return to the situation existing in the fifties. The risks have multiplied. The mere potential for destruction available today poses an immense threat to security in times of heightened tension. Moreover, numerous regional crises run the risk of becoming major conflagrations.

Let us then make sure that we are never discouraged. However painful setbacks may be, they are no reason for turning back. The important thing is to learn from our experience, including our mistakes, and to stay on course for our true destination: peace and cooperation. Let us free ourselves from illusions, but let us by all means remain steadfast.

The third factor in the global changes taking place, and hence the third new task for the decade ahead of us, consists in reshaping relations between industrialized and developing countries, between North and South. In fact, this much-used term "North-South" conveys an inadequate idea of the complexity of highly differing levels of development and gravely imbalanced relations between rich and poor peoples, between richer and poorer nations.

It is certainly no exaggeration on my part when I say that I regard this imbalance as *the* social challenge of our times. Today, one-fifth of mankind is already suffering hunger and malnutrition: 800 million people are living a life of "absolute poverty," to use the customary international terminology. The bulk of these men and women live in Southeast Asia and the sub-Saharan regions of Africa. During the last decade they have hardly made any progress at all. If no fundamental changes take place, the 1980s will prove no better. By the end of the millenium, the world's population will have grown to over six billion people. Eighty-five percent of this total will be living in what are now the developing countries. Even if their birthrate declines, a country like Tanzania will have more inhabitants by the year 2000 than Canada with her wide expanses of land and abundance of resources.

A reduction in population growth forms one of the first priorities if we are to prevent the disastrous depletion of the world's natural resources. Naturally, that alone will not suffice.

But it forms a necessary pre-condition for any comprehensive solutions for overcoming mass poverty.

In view of these challenges, it is not surprising that pessimism and resignation are spreading. However, such reactions provide a poor guide for action. In my opinion, we in America and Europe have the ability to cope with the difficulties, but we will probably face setbacks before making serious progress.

We must understand, and make others understand, that there is no longer room for a gross materialism which, in any case, does not go well with a democratic *raison d'etat*. European social democrats certainly are not pleading the virtue of high-minded renunciation: they are pleading the case for social justice and fair treatment, both within states and between states.

In a period of deep-rooted and rapid changes, we shall only survive if individual interests are embedded within an overall framework of social solidarity. Democratic socialists do not need to undergo a process of relearning in this respect. Individual freedom is worth little if it does not rest on freedom for all. A free and democratic system can only stand if it succeeds in creating and justifying fresh confidence on the part of the whole community. It follows that government must prove sensitive to those affected by its decisions. Successful economic and social policy requires as much coordination as possible between political decision-making, enterprise and the trade unions.

Moreover, the holders of political office—especially those with a background in democratic socialism—should remain receptive to fresh ideas. The search for alternative life-styles must not be simply dismissed as either a fanciful or sinister attack on the established political order. Present-day conditions leave us no choice than to seek more actively for solutions to the worrisome economic and ecological problems of our time.

The challenges I am referring to are greater than the capacity of any one nation, including America. As for Europe, it seems to me that this old continent of ours could once more find the strength to seriously promote peaceful conditions in this world. To accomplish that, it must first overcome its persistent inner strife. These difficult times, however, do not exactly facilitate the historic attempt to forge a new European unit out of the old independent traditions. Some of the ambitious projects contemplated in the early seventies have had to be postponed. Instead, we have focussed our attention on consolidating what has already been achieved.

What does it mean in black and white when we talk of making headway in European cooperation and unification? To begin with, the European community must resolve its present economic and political problems before undertaking an enlargement that might include Greece, Spain and Portugal. The structures which hardly sufficed for a community of six and then proved inadequate for the Europe of nine will have to be fundamentally reformed for a well-functioning twelve-state community.

A close relationship between North America and Europe remains an indispensable foundation of peace. Naturally, these relations are also subject to dynamic movements. The pattern of power no longer corresponds to what it was immediately after the war. And not all the experiences which the United States has meanwhile undergone seem to us in Europe worthy of imitation. Yet the problems confronting the United States and Europe are essentially the same. The quest for quality of life for working people, the efforts to bring about an adequate educational system, the safeguarding of energy supplies and the rehabilitation of decaying city centres: these among others are all subjects which preoccupy our American friends every bit as much as they do the Europeans. For that reason, we ought to strengthen our mutual exchange of views and experience, particularly among the young generation. It might help if we pressed ahead with the establishment of those youth exchange programs which proved so useful in promoting friendly relations between other peoples. I am thinking especially of the Franco-German youth program.

The European nations, however, cannot decrease world tensions on their own. The leaders of the two superpowers must discharge their supreme responsibilities towards other nations and create that minimum of confidence without which predictability is impossible. Otherwise there will be no end to the arms race; without an end to the arms race, detente (relaxation of tensions) cannot last; and without detente there can be no reliable security. The issue is not one of settling technical questions, however important that may be in specific cases. The real issue lies in summoning up the political will for arms limitation. Without that, politics will lose the race against technology. And that seems just another way of saying that the human race is unable to control in political terms its full technological potential.

Preparatory talks on the limitation of theater nuclear weapons indicate that the period of complete inactivity might be drawing to a close. It should also prove possible to implement the provisions included in the SALT II Treaty—whose symbolic importance consists in the equal status accorded to the two nuclear superpowers—and to start serious negotiations on SALT III; then a measure of guarded optimism may again be warranted.

I do not belong to those who expect wonders from the Conference on Security and Cooperation. In many cases, the consequences of the division of Europe are still painful even five years after Helsinki. But it is worth the effort of continuing to speak with each other and to negotiate to achieve progress—however small it may be. Europe has long since ceased to be the hub of the world, but it remains of decisive importance that we in Europe maintain peace and thereby furnish an example of how differing interests can be reconciled without explosive conflicts. The Brandt Commission Report sets out detailed proposals for what should be done and what can realistically be accomplished. Many of its recommendations will not be translatable into practice for some time. Others may be overtaken by events or fresh challenges. Nevertheless, we should bear four central priorities in mind when determining our objectives for the next five years. First, a major transfer of resources to the developing countries, which will help stimulate world trade. Second, a global strategy on energy supplies. Third, the overcoming of mass hunger. Fourth, a sweeping reform of those international institutions concerned with developmental, economic and financial questions.

The coming year will provide several occasions for achieving progress in North-South relations. We must hope for rapid progress from the "global negotiations" to begin in New York in early 1981. The world economic summit in Canada will provide the leading industrial nations another opportunity to demonstrate a more constructive response to the demands of developing countries. But even before that conference, a number of international measures will prove necessary to deal with the alarming balance-of-payments difficulties in a number of developing countries.

Next year will hopefully also see an ad-hoc and selective summit meeting between leading statesmen from North and South. I have the impression that the soundings taken by Austria and Mexico are meeting with a favorable response. And it would be most helpful if the United States could take part in this project.

I hope it has become clear that I am not prophesying the decline of the West. And I have no intention of creating an atmosphere of crisis. I wanted to address what we must jointly seek to accomplish: awareness of our position; a sense of reality about the world in which we live; and hard work to find answers to the questions now besetting us and, moreover, no longer so very new.

In my opinion, many political debates and many election campaigns simply bypass a discussion of the crucial issues. Our democracies are judged by many citizens in terms of their ability to shape the future actively and constructively. If the impression were to prevail that traditional politicians merely react to external events instead of shaping them, then it is hardly surprising if unconventional or even dangerous ideas start to spread. The experience gained during recent years has pointed to the dimension of the challenges now drawing near. In future, we must bear in mind better than hitherto—and act accordingly—that international security is not only a question of military power. That may be becoming less and less the case. But in addition, it is becoming more and more unmistakably a question of social peace, of adequate innovation and of an equitable balance of interests. And that applies to domestic as well as foreign policy. At any rate, that seems to me to be the common belief held by most of those representing democratic socialism.

We live in a common world marked by a shortage of resources and a steady growth in the problems confronting us. Our most precious assets are human inventiveness and social responsibility. And it is these qualities which the peoples of the world must call to mind as they become fully aware of their mutual dependence.

Index